Interpretation of Contracts

How far should it be possible for courts, through the process of interpretation, to control the bargain made between parties? Are judges applying the principles of interpretation in the same way? What is the relevant context of an agreement? Should contracting parties be able to opt out of a particular interpretative approach by use of mechanisms such as entire agreement clauses?

Many contract disputes ultimately turn upon the meaning attributed to contractual documents by judges. Lord Hoffman's judgment in *Investors Compensation Scheme v West Bromwich Building Society* included a modern restatement of the rules of interpretation to be applied by the courts which favoured a more contextual approach to contractual interpretation. This judgment has generated controversy within the legal profession and sparked academic debate on a previously neglected topic. This short book examines what contextual interpretation means, the arguments for and against contextual interpretation, and suggests ways in which the parties may be able to influence the interpretation methods applied to their agreement.

Examining case law, academic debate and the resurgence of interest in formalist contract interpretation in the US, this text identifies the controversial issues, explores the range of arguments and analyses possible future developments.

Catherine Mitchell is Senior Lecturer in Law at the University of Hull.

Interpretation of Contracts

Current controversies in law

Catherine Mitchell

Routledge·Cavendish
Taylor & Francis Group
LONDON AND NEW YORK

First published 2007
by Routledge-Cavendish
2 Park Square, Milton Park, Abingdon, Oxon OX14 4RN, UK

Simultaneously published in the USA and Canada
by Routledge-Cavendish
270 Madison Ave, New York, NY 10016

Routledge-Cavendish is an imprint of the Taylor & Francis Group, an
informa business

Typeset in Times by
RefineCatch Limited, Bungay, Suffolk
Printed and bound in Great Britain by
Antony Rowe Ltd, Chippenham, Wiltshire

British Library Cataloguing in Publication Data
A catalogue record for this book is available from the British Library

Library of Congress Cataloging in Publication Data
Mitchell, Catherine.
    Interpretation of contracts / Catherine Mitchell.
        p. cm.
    ISBN 978-1-84568-044-2 (pbk.)
    1. Contracts – Great Britain – Interpretation and construction.
I. Title.
    KD1554.M58 2007
    346.4102 – dc22   2006039512

ISBN10: 0-415-44777-1 (hbk.)
ISBN10: 1-84568-044-8 (pbk.)
ISBN10: 0-203-94520-4 (ebk.)

ISBN13: 978-0-415-44777-5 (hbk.)
ISBN13: 978-1-84568-044-2 (pbk.)
ISBN13: 978-0-203-94520-9 (ebk.)

Dedicated to Kitty and the memory of Keith

Contents

Table of cases

Preface

This book examines the controversies that surround the question of
how contracts should be interpreted by courts, that is, how the courts
decide the meaning of a contract, and identify the obligations the
parties have undertaken to each other. It is not intended to be a
comprehensive statement of interpretation rules applied by courts,
nor does it attempt to analyse all the doctrines of contract law that
might be reckoned to be 'interpretative' in one sense or another. I
have tried to consider some issues that seem to have been neglected
by others working in the field, such as the extent to which the parties
can influence the courts' interpretative method. I also try to identify
the factors that have been, or are likely to become, material in influencing contracts interpretation. The book therefore seeks to present
an overview of the subject, rather than a detailed analysis of all its
aspects, and I hope it will serve as a useful introduction for those
who are relatively new to contract law, and who might wonder why
interpretation matters, as well as being of interest to scholars and
practitioners.

My friends and colleagues at the Law School, University of Hull,
and elsewhere, have provided support, advice and assistance of various kinds while I have been engaged on the book. I would like to
thank in particular Bev Clucas, Fiona Cownie, Gerry Johnstone,
Peter Paulden and Tony Ward. I am very grateful to Christian
Twigg-Flesner, who read the entire work in draft, and offered many
helpful suggestions and comments. Some of the material in chapters
four and five is based upon an article of mine, 'Entire Agreement
Clauses: Contracting Out of Contextualism', which appeared in
the 2006 volume of the *Journal of Contract Law*. I am grateful to
Professor John Carter for his assistance. Finally, I thank Alex and
Tom for their patience, encouragement and sense of humour.

Chapter 1

The nature and scope of contractual interpretation

Introduction

What is contractual interpretation and how do courts carry it out? This short book examines these related and controversial questions. Much recent work on the subject has been prompted by Lord Hoffmann's restatement of the principles of contractual interpretation in *Investors Compensation Scheme v West Bromwich Building Society*.[1] As has been noted by many, despite the practical importance of interpretation in contract disputes, the subject was largely ignored by contract scholars prior to the *Investors* judgment. This might have been because of the belief that the subject could be reduced to a few simple 'rules of construction', the main rule being that words in the contract should be interpreted according to their plain, natural or ordinary meaning. Lord Hoffmann's restatement has become a point of focus because he articulated a shift away from this simplistic approach in favour of contextual interpretation.[2] This contextual method is variously described as involving reference to the 'background' or 'factual matrix' of the contract, or the 'reasonable expectations of the parties', or the 'commercial purposes' of the agreement or 'business common sense'. These would seem to be just different ways of saying the same thing: that contractual interpretation is not just a process of unreflectingly grasping the plain meaning of the words of the contractual text and applying them to the facts of the dispute, but involves a wider examination of the contractual circumstances, which might include almost any information relevant

---

1   [1998] 1 All ER 98.
2   Ibid., pp 114–15. See also the statement from Lord Steyn in *Sirius International Insurance Company v FAI General Insurance Ltd* [2004] UKHL 54 at [19].

to understanding the agreement, with one or two notable exceptions. In short, contractual interpretation must now be understood as an inclusive rather than an exclusive process.

The *Investors* decision is almost 10 years old and now would seem to be a good time to take an overview of its impact and influence. Most contract scholars are broadly supportive of the change in direction in interpretation – even arguing that it does not go far enough – whereas practitioners and some judges have been more guarded. Whether there has been any significant change in direction by the courts is a matter of dispute – the transformation in interpretative method may be more apparent than real.[3] But it is not clear that anything of great significance turns on the debate over whether the contextual approach is really novel or whether Lord Hoffmann can claim credit for authoring the change. Rather, while the shift to the contextual approach *appears* to be controversial, the exact lines of the debate are difficult to draw. For example, the obvious controversy in contractual interpretation is over the existence and role of plain or literal meaning, since some will argue that the plain meaning approach should not be displaced by contextual interpretation.[4] But it is certainly a mistake to regard 'contextual' and 'literal' interpretation as polar opposites, or as the only two possible techniques in contractual interpretation. Identifying the genuine debates requires close attention to the questions of what contractual interpretation is, when it is required and what the purposes of it are. The book will not necessarily take judicial pronouncements on interpretation at face value. Rather, it will try to draw out the substance of the changes that have taken place in an attempt to uncover the areas of agreement and controversy in contractual interpretation. In doing so, it will address matters that have so far been largely ignored by contract scholars, such as whether and how interpretation can be distinguished from other tasks a court might undertake, whether it is possible for the parties to control the interpretative method applied to their agreement and the 'context' of the shift to contextual interpretation.

There are two points to make at the outset. First, my concern is with commercial contractual interpretation, rather than consumer

---

3 For example, see the statement from the trial judge in *Mitsubishi Corp v Eastwind Transport* [2004] EWHC 2924 at [28].

4 See for example, Davenport, B.J., 'Thanks to the House of Lords' (1999) 115 *LQR* 11.

contracting. The latter, characterised as it often is by inequality of bargaining power, raises particular issues that cannot be dealt with here. In relation to consumer contracting, interpretation of terms cannot be the whole story, as policy issues concerning fairness and transparency of terms are also important. Second, the book is not concerned with attempting comprehensive coverage of all the issues and cases in relation to contractual interpretation. Rather, it attempts to concentrate on fewer cases in more detail, and particular areas of difficulty or disagreement.

In the remainder of this chapter the notions of 'interpretation' and 'contract' will be examined more fully. Some introductory points concerning contractual controversies and contractual power will be made. The question of whether it is possible to distinguish interpretation from other techniques, which a court might apply to an agreement to extract its meaning, will also be explored. The range of interpretative problems that arise, and some of the reasons *why* interpretation disputes arise, will be discussed. The overall aim of this chapter is to demonstrate the difficulties of reining in the ideas of both 'contract' and 'interpretation'. The resulting pervasiveness of contextual contractual interpretation has potential implications for the balance of power between judges and the parties. More specifically, it is possible to perceive 'contextual interpretation' as operating on two different levels. The first level is in relation to 'meanings of words' problems in the contractual documents. This is the most familiar area for the operation of 'context' in contract. But the second, broader level is in relation to assessing the contractual relationship and contractual obligations as a whole. In this broader sense, contextualism involves examining a wider range of materials, not only to assist in interpreting the words of the agreement, but also to assist in understanding the entire contractual relationship, including, but not limited to, deciding what the parties were trying to achieve by their agreement. If contextual interpretation cannot be confined to the process of just discovering the meaning of words, it arguably becomes easier to use the process of 'contextual interpretation' to justify a departure from those words.

Chapter 2 will consider the 'contextual' approach to contracts in greater detail, scrutinising Lord Hoffmann's dicta in *Investors* and the subsequent case law. Chapter 3 considers some of the problems that arise from the contextual approach, such as the availability of multiple contexts for an agreement, and the role of plain meaning. Chapter 4 considers what is often taken to be the alternative to contextualism, some variety of formalism in contractual interpretation. Chapter 5 examines whether and how the parties might have some control over the interpretative method adopted by a court. The broad argument is that, given the courts are required to balance an increasing number of considerations in contractual interpretation, there should be greater scope for the parties to control, or at least influence, the choice of interpretative method applied to their agreement.

What is interpretation?

This basic question is perhaps the most difficult one to answer at the outset, since 'interpretation' is, by its nature, an elusive concept. It is difficult to advance any widely accepted view of what interpretation is and how it should be conducted, since almost everything claimed in relation to interpretation is disputed. Indeed, disputes about the general concept of interpretation account for many of the controversies surrounding contractual interpretation, although this may not always be recognised. Similarly, explaining a 'contract' is not always as straightforward as it might appear. Nevertheless, some preliminary points need to be made. Before that, though, a brief word about terminology needs to be given. Debates in interpretation generally manifest themselves between different 'camps'. Thus there is the 'textualist' (or literalist), who approaches the interpretative task with a belief that the text is largely self-sufficient and can be interpreted without reference to any extrinsic evidence. The textualist may be at odds with both 'contextualists' and 'intentionalists' in interpretation. Contextualism is broadly the position that material other than the text is important to the interpretative task, and intentionalism is the position that interpretation involves the search for author's intent. Despite the possibility for a neat classification, there is a potential source of confusion here, since while one can contrast the 'textualist' with a 'contextualist', one can also refer to *contextual meanings of a text* contrasted with literal, ordinary, plain or natural meanings of a text. In contract, contextual interpretation is usually the process of fixing upon contextual meanings of the words of the text. Hence, the common opposing positions are usually described as between 'literalists' and 'contextualists' or 'literalists' and 'purposivists'. This means that 'contextualism' cannot always be fully distinguished from 'textualism', where this latter word signifies a belief in the freestanding nature of texts. The difficulty is that 'contextualism' may also express the position of scepticism that the contractual text should carry much weight at all in the identification of the parties' obligations. In other words, there is a version of contextualism in contract that denies the central importance of the text.[5] This is discussed more fully below, but one needs to sound a note of caution, since participants in interpretation debates do not all use the same terminology, nor do they all necessarily mean the same thing by 'contextualism' or 'contextual interpretation'. It will generally be apparent from the discussion which particular position is referred to, and the words literal, ordinary, plain, conventional or natural meaning will be used more or less interchangeably, unless otherwise indicated.

A general theory of interpretation?

The difficulties we may face in explaining the nature of contractual interpretation reflect wider debates about what interpretation means and how it should be undertaken in other areas – in literature and the arts for example. The fact that interpretation operates across many different activities and contexts causes some scholars to doubt whether any general theory of interpretation of texts – whether legal, literary or other – is either possible or desirable. Sunstein, for example, writes, 'Interpretive practices are highly dependent on context and on role, and by abstracting from context and role, any theory is likely to prove uninformatively broad, or to go badly wrong in particular cases.'[6] Many such differences suggested by 'context' and 'role' are, of course, immediately apparent. So, for example, 'interpretations of legal texts invoke coercive state power, while interpretations of literary texts do not'.[7] Similarly, a contract evidently stands in a different position to a statute, since it only has coercive power over the parties to it and only then to the extent that they invoke the law to assist in enforcement. The point is, that the meaning to be extracted from contractual documents may not be just a function of the application of any particular interpretative theory, but depends upon the values that judges take contract law to embody, together

---

5   Collins, H., 'Objectivity and Committed Contextualism in Interpretation', in S. Worthington (ed.) *Commercial Law and Commercial Practice*, 2003, Oxford: Hart, pp 189, 192 (hereafter 'Committed Contextualism').

6   Sunstein, C., *Legal Reasoning and Political Conflict*, New York: OUP, 1996, p 167.

7   Baron, J., 'Law, Literature and the Problems of Interdisciplinarity' (1999) 108 *Yale LJ* 1059, 1080.

with their view of law's role in regulating market activity. 'Contract interpretation' is a conduit through which these wider considerations can be channelled and applied to particular agreements. Outcomes are therefore not wholly interpretation-led but are, to an extent, policy- and value-led. Despite these objections, examining the general notion of 'interpretation' will allow us to get some grasp, however tenuous, of the subject of our enquiry. In addition, an examination of the nature of interpretation will illustrate that some of the controversies over contractual interpretation reflect wider debates in interpretative theory and legal theory more generally.

Interpretation and meaning

'Interpretation' is usually the label applied to the process of uncovering meaning and seeking to understand an object in a situation where there is some doubt or room for difference of opinion.[8] One important – perhaps definitive – distinction is that interpretation is an activity undertaken in relation to an object or practice already existing, and the form of that object or practice will be a constraint upon the interpretations that can be applied to it.[9] How much of a constraint the original object is, and how much freedom the interpreter has to create something new, are matters of dispute. But the very usefulness of the concept of interpretation is often thought to lie in its capturing these elements of both freedom and restraint. So the concept of interpretation has attracted theorists seeking an alternative explanation to untrammelled judicial discretion to create law in cases where legal rules appear to have run out.[10] The existence of an 'object' to be interpreted does mean that interpretation and creation can be understood as qualitatively distinct processes, even if on occasion it becomes difficult to tell precisely where one ends and the other begins. This distinction is very familiar in contract law, where judges frequently deny any power to create a contract for the parties, only the power to interpret the agreement already made in accordance with the parties' intentions. The need to demonstrate constraints may also explain the courts' preference for the contractual text, when available, as the object to be interpreted. In relation to the outcomes of interpretation, this is usually to provide an

---

8 MacCormick, N., *Rhetoric and the Rule of Law*, 2005, Oxford: OUP, pp 121–2.
9 Dworkin, R., *Law's Empire*, 1986, London: Fontana, p 66.
10 Ibid., Dworkin.

explanation of the object, which deepens understanding of it or presents some original insight into it. In relation to contractual obligation, the idea of the end point is important – one does not really interpret the contract just to gain 'insight' into it, but to determine a practical point with important implications: what obligations have the contracting parties undertaken to each other?[11] Interpretation of the agreement may therefore be a necessary part of resolving the dispute. Dispute resolution is the primary aim of the judge in the contract case.

Associating the process of interpretation with uncovering meaning – at least where the subject of interpretation is language – does not necessarily take us very far. Andrei Marmor writes that 'roughly, interpretation can be defined as an understanding or explanation of the meaning of an object'.[12] But he goes on to point out that 'meaning' itself has various meanings. In relation to language, he distinguishes semantics – 'those aspects of (linguistic) communication which are rule or convention governed'[13] – from interpretation, which is required 'because the issue is not determined by rules or conventions'.[14] Marmor writes that 'understanding or explaining the meaning of an expression and interpreting it, are two conceptually separate things'.[15] Thus provided my friend and I share the same conventional understanding of the colour that people in our community generally call 'black', and the animal that such people call 'a cat', she can understand my meaning, arguably without any interpretation, when I say, 'My cat is black'. There are those legal scholars that support the idea of conventional or plain meaning, at least in relation to the operation of some rules.[16] Most famously, H. L. A. Hart drew a distinction between the core of certainty of a rule's application, and the penumbra of doubt that arose because of the 'open texture' of language.[17] For some theorists then, interpretation is a 'parasitic activity' that depends upon, but is essentially distinguishable from, other activities, such as identifying the practice or object,

---

11 Smith, S., *Contract Theory*, 2004, Oxford: OUP, p 271.
12 Marmor, A., *Interpretation and Legal Theory*, 2nd edn, 2005, Oxford: Hart, p 9.
13 Ibid., Marmor, p 15.
14 Ibid. (emphasis in the original).
15 Ibid., Marmor, p 17.
16 For example, Hart, H.L.A., *The Concept of Law*, 2nd edn, 1994, Oxford: OUP; Ibid., Marmor; Schauer, F., *Playing by the Rules*, 1991, Oxford: OUP, ch 9.
17 Ibid., Hart, p 123.

or fixing upon a basic understanding or meaning of it.[18] For such a theorist, interpretation is a higher-level form of inquiry, which takes over when 'understanding' yields no, or conflicting, answers.[19]

This fairly innocuous idea that interpretation involves uncovering meaning in situations of doubt is itself disputed, since it suggests that there is no need for interpretation where meaning is clear, that is, when plain meaning of a text can be grasped. The issue of whether we can ever fix upon meaning without an act of interpretation, if texts can ever be said to have 'plain meanings' that are not based upon some interpretative criteria, is one that is hotly contested, both in the realm of interpretation theory and legal theory. For some theorists, *all* questions about meaning are concerned with interpretation because there is *always* room for doubt. There can be no instant grasp of plain meaning that does not involve an act of interpretation, however unreflectingly this act might be undertaken. The notion of 'context' is important to this wider view of interpretation, since it is the availability of multiple contexts for communication that makes interpretation necessary. Stanley Fish, for example, writes that:

> A sentence is never not in a context. We are never not in a situation. A statute is never not read in the light of some purpose. A set of interpretive assumptions is always in force. A sentence that seems to need no interpretation is already the product of one.[20]

The argument here is that even when only conventional meaning is relied upon, the importance of context is still apparent – no text, or communication, can be self-sufficient in relation to how it is to be interpreted. This wide view of interpretation has the potential to expand considerably what can be achieved through a process of 'contextual interpretation'. Since much depends here on what an appeal to 'context' means, this concept must be considered in more detail.

Context and interpretation

Contexts can be broad or narrow and can be restricted or expanded to exclude or include relevant information. Contextual interpretation in

18 Patterson, D., 'Interpretation in Law' (2005) 42 *San Diego LR* 685, 686.
19 Ibid., Patterson, pp 688–90.
20 Fish, S., *Is There a Text in this Class?*, 1980, Cambridge, Mass: Harvard UP, p 284.

contract has been described as no more than 'concentric circles working outwards, ever increasing in scope: word, phrase, sentence, paragraph, clause, section of contract, whole contract, surrounding factual matrix, legal and commercial context'.[21] Contractual contexts can, of course, be drawn much wider. Consider this conception of context from Charles Fried: 'Promises, like every human expression are made against an unexpressed background of shared purposes, experience and even a shared theory of the world. Without such a common background communication would be impossible'.[22] In contract then, context encompasses the whole range of information from the rest of the phrase to 'a shared theory of the world'. Given the breadth of context, it is easy to conclude that there is always some context operating. It therefore becomes crucial to choose the correct context within which to interpret an utterance or communication. The fact that there is always a context has two particular implications for contractual interpretation.

First, we may all agree that meaning is always contextual, but disagree over what is the correct context, over how much context is relevant or necessary to accessing meaning, and precisely why the contextual meaning is sought – is it to uphold the intentions of the parties, or to achieve an economically efficient outcome, or something else? A textualist (here meaning a person who regards commitment to the plain meaning of the words of a contractual text as the paramount concern in interpretation) will almost certainly concede that some context is operating, but that the context may be so wide – a common language, a shared currency, a shared background knowledge of the legal rules – that articulating it as the relevant 'background' may not assist in fixing on an interpretation that is supported by the text, does not defeat commercial purpose and satisfactorily resolves the dispute. In addition, there are many different contexts within which an agreement can be placed: a strict legal context or the context of a 30-year contracting history between the parties?[23] Different judges can claim to be taking a contextual approach to interpretation, but have very different views about what an appeal to 'context' entails.

---

21 McMeel, G., 'The Rise of Commercial Construction in Contract Law' [1998] *Lloyds MCLQ* 382, 388, paraphrasing Clarke, M., *The Law of Insurance Contracts*, 3rd edn, 1997, London: LLP, para 15–3.
22 Fried, C., *Contract as Promise*, 1981, Cambridge, Mass: Harvard UP, p 88.
23 See facts of *Baird Textiles Ltd v Marks and Spencer plc* [2001] EWCA Civ 274.

Second, it may be perfectly permissible to adopt a plain meaning approach, or to rely on the text at the expense of other evidence, but only to the extent that such an approach is required by the context of the agreement. Hugh Collins points out that the 'literal meaning of context is "not text" and that while "[t]ext matters", to be sure, . . . how much it matters depends upon context.'[24] This shifts the focus of the debate from being one concerned with text versus context, to one where the text can be undermined (or supported) by context. Given the width of possible contexts, therefore, it is not the case that contextualism always stands in opposition to textualism and literalism. To accept the central role of context in interpretation does not make plain meaning redundant – it relocates literalism as a possible interpretative strategy that operates within a broader contextualism. This possibility is considered further in Chapters 2 and 4.

The idea of 'context' then, like the notion of 'interpretation', is difficult to confine. In that case, what are we to make of 'contextual interpretation' in contract? On one hand, provided a judge is engaged in the process of *interpretation* (more narrowly defined), s/he can access a particular set of justificatory arguments that are reconcilable with the view that contractual obligations are created voluntarily by the parties. To regard a process as involving 'interpretation' generally lends legitimacy to the judge's work: 'Viewing judging as limited to the task of interpretation casts judges as conduits who transmit the law rather than as sources of law who necessarily possess the discretion to make it'.[25] Constraint is also suggested by the possibility of 'plain' or 'conventional' meanings. The idea that words have plain meanings seems particularly important in contract law since it is arguably *only* the belief in the possibility of ordinary (or literal, conventional, plain, natural or linguistic) meaning that makes communication about entitlements and obligations between different persons possible – and makes it plausible to have a neutral third-party referee any disputes (at least at relatively low cost). On this basis it ought to be possible to posit meanings that are not 'open to interpretation'.

On the other hand, the realisation that some context is always operating, together with the availability of multiple contexts within which words can be analysed, threatens to turn 'interpretation' into an activity that engulfs the whole process of ascertaining meaning

24 Op. cit., Collins, 'Committed Contextualism', pp 192, 193.
25 McGowan, M., 'Against Interpretation' (2005) 42 *San Diego LR* 711, 733.

in all instances of communication. One problem with this is the possibility of infinite regress: if all meaning and understanding is attributable to some act of interpretation then there can be no noninterpretative starting point for inquiry. The nature of the interpretative task must also be a question of interpretation and so on – 'we are simply driven back in our search, stage after stage, *ad infinitum*'.[26] Understandings of the practice would be endlessly disputed and meaningful constraints would be absent. Texts become inherently unstable and unreliable.[27] There are strategies to overcome this, such as to posit a 'right' method of interpretation, which yields a correct outcome,[28] or to make the understandings of an 'interpretative community' the starting point,[29] but these raise their own difficulties. In terms of contractual interpretation, if all instances of determining meaning are 'interpretations', if interpretation is always contextual and if there is no obvious limit on the contextual information, there is arguably greater scope for imputing doubt over what the contractual words mean and a greater possibility for interfering in the contract under the guise of 'interpreting' it. Part of the difficulty here lies in the breadth of the project of 'contractual interpretation'. If the point of contractual interpretation is to determine what obligations the parties owe to each other, it is difficult to confine this to a close analysis of the words of a contractual text. It is particularly difficult if these enquiries are contextual, since this may uncover information that suggests that the text was not that important to the parties' agreement. The contextual interpretative issue may then shift to a consideration of the precise *role* of the documents in the parties' relationship. Thus while it might be preferable to rein in the idea of contractual interpretation, practically, this is a difficult thing to do, since a broader view of interpretation would seem to put the contractual text under threat. This will become clearer in the next section, when the idea of 'a contract' is examined.

26 Simmonds, N.E., 'Imperial Visions and Mundane Practices' [1987] *CLJ* 465, 472. On infinite regress see also op. cit., Patterson, 'Interpretation in Law', p 690.
27 Binder, G. and Weisberg, R., *Literary Criticisms of Law*, 2000, New Jersey: Princeton University Press, p 28.
28 Op. cit., Dworkin's strategy in *Law's Empire*.
29 Op. cit., Fish, S., *Is There a Text in this Class?*.

What is a contract?

In contractual interpretation, what exactly is it that we are seeking to interpret? The contract may be the formal, relatively comprehensive written document, containing the terms, conditions and signatures, but most modern scholars with an appreciation of literature from the social sciences regard it as something more elusive – the agreement the parties make, which may or may not be the same thing as the documents.[30] Indeed, textualist interpretation, which concentrates on the text of the contractual documents, would seem to face two related difficulties. The first is that lawyers, rather than the contracting parties, draft many formal contractual documents, so there may be doubt about how far the contractual text is authoritative as a statement of the *parties'* intentions.[31] Interpretative difficulties often turn on the 'small print' of standard terms and conditions, which usually go unread by the contracting parties.[32] The second is that the documents may be an unreliable record of the parties' agreement. The contractual text may not reflect all the parties' understandings about their obligations and their relationship, and may be written in fairly technical 'legal' language. Although legal mechanisms are available to the court to remedy these defects, and enforce the agreement according to the parties' 'reasonable expectations', contractual interpretation tends towards textualism in that it is usually directed to some written provision in the contractual documents. This can often make contractual interpretation a rather artificial exercise. Lord Hoffmann recognised this when he wrote, extrajudicially, 'the people whose utterances have to be interpreted by the courts are often to a greater or lesser extent imaginary'.[33] Artificiality results from both the pre-eminence the law attaches to the view of 'reasonable persons', rather than the actual contracting parties in interpretation, and their attachment to written documents. English law is committed to the objective theory of agreement, which prioritises the outward expressions and manifest signs of the contract rather

---

30 For example Linzer, P., 'The Comfort of Certainty: Plain Meaning and the Parol Evidence Rule' (2002) 71 *Fordham LR* 799, 822.

31 Collins, H., *Regulating Contracts*, 1999, Oxford: OUP, pp 153–4, 159.

32 Courts frequently recognise this; see, for example, the comments of Mance LJ in *Sinochem International Oil (London) Co Ltd v Mobil Sales and Supply Corporation* [2000] 1 Lloyd's Rep 339, [28].

33 Lord Hoffmann, 'The Intolerable Wrestle with Words and Meanings' (1997) 114 *SALJ* 656, 661, hereafter 'Intolerable Wrestle'.

than any inner intentions. The attachment to documents is reinforced by the operation of the parol evidence rule, which dictates that where a contract is in writing, it may not be varied by extrinsic evidence of its terms. Although there are numerous inroads into this doctrine, it has recently been reasserted at the highest level.[34]

This identification of the contract with the documents has been questioned.[35] Insights gained from a sociolegal appreciation of contractual obligations suggest that while the legal framework to the contract is important, the extent of its importance – particularly to the contracting parties, as opposed to their lawyers – should not be overemphasised. In *Regulating Contracts*,[36] for example, Collins takes a sceptical view about the relevance of the legal contract and contract law rules to the agreement the parties make. In his view, the legal rules and decisions in cases frequently undermine the reasonable expectations of the parties which, in the commercial context, are based on 'considerations of the long term business relation, the customs of the trade, and the success of the deal'[37] rather than the contractual planning documents. For Collins, protection of reasonable expectations involves a contextual approach to contractual disputes, not sole reliance on the closed system of legal rules.[38] He writes that reasonable expectation is a 'broader, open-textured standard' that can be utilised to 'expand the range of information that will describe the standards governing the contractual arrangement'.[39] It is the social framework, or context, of agreements that gives rise to most of the contracting parties' intentions and expectations, not the legal regulation.[40] Some judges are aware of the limitations of the written contract in this regard, often revealing anecdotally that contracting parties seem to care little about the legal

---

34 Per Lord Hobhouse, *Shogun Finance Ltd v Hudson* [2003] UKHL 62, [2003] 3 WLR 1371, p 1386.
35 Op. cit., Linzer; Macaulay, S., 'The Real Deal and the Paper Deal: Empirical Pictures of Relationships, Complexity and the Urge for Transparent Simple Rules' (hereafter 'Real Deal') in D. Campbell, H. Collins and J. Wightman (eds) *Implicit Dimensions of Contract*, 2003, Oxford: Hart, (hereafter *Implicit Dimensions*), p 51 at 53–6; Collins, *Regulating Contracts*, ch 6.
36 Op. cit.
37 Ibid., p 271.
38 Ibid., pp 146–8.
39 Ibid., p 146.
40 See op. cit., Macaulay, S., 'Real Deal'.

documents.[41] Faced with the criticism that the law is simply irrelevant to most transactions, it seems the effectiveness of contract law can no longer be measured by its certainty in promulgating and enforcing a strict body of doctrinal rules, but by its success in supporting and upholding the more elusive 'reasonable expectations of the parties'.[42]

The realisation of the importance of the social framework may have been one of the motivating factors behind the recent change in interpretative emphasis. The view of many notionally 'commercial contractors' may be that legal contracts and contract law get in the way of doing business.[43] Certainly, arguments along such lines are starting to appear in the cases. In *Balmoral Group Ltd v Borealis (UK) Ltd*, for example, counsel for Balmoral had argued in front of Clarke J that:

> there were, in effect two parallel universes: the 'real world' in which the parties moved and had their being, and an artificial world created for them by their lawyers when, but only when, a dispute arose. In the real world, as he submits, none of the individuals who were doing business with each other on behalf of Balmoral and Borealis paid any attention to the terms and conditions that the lawyers had drafted for them . . . It was only when the lawyers came on the scene that the parties were transposed to an artificial world where reliance was placed on standard terms . . .[44]

To take the written documents as the ultimate expression of the parties' will, and as the object to be interpreted, may therefore be at variance with the realities of the agreement. This increasing sensitivity to whether the documents really capture all the parties' understandings about their agreement has the potential to turn contextual interpretation into a much more expansive project. It may prove difficult to confine contractual interpretation to the task of

41 Lord Devlin, 'The Relationship between Commercial Law and Commercial Practice' (1951) 14 *MLR* 249, p 252.
42 Lord Steyn, 'Contract Law: Fulfilling the Reasonable Expectations of Honest Men' (1997) 113 *LQR* 433.
43 Op. cit., Lord Devlin, 252; Beale, H. and Dugdale, T., 'Contracts between Businessmen: Planning and the Use of Contractual Remedies' (1975) 2 *British Journal of Law and Society* 45, 47–8.
44 [2006] EWHC 1900, at para [339]. See also Collins, *Regulating Contracts*, p 155.

uncovering the meaning of the words in the documents, since contextual interpretation may also provide information that gives rise to doubts that the contractual text is an accurate reflection of the parties' obligations. In other words, it may be that the genuine agreement cannot be yielded from the documents at all.

It might be argued that there is a common misunderstanding evidenced here. Schauer has written that confusion is often displayed between two different questions: what should one do in relation to a difficult case and what does the text mean? The latter is rightly an interpretative issue, but the former is not, although it will often be presented as one.[45] Thus there is a distinction between the task of giving effect to understandings and expectations generated outside the contract by contractual means – techniques such as implied contracts, implied terms, collateral contracts and so on – and using contextual material (factual background, commercial purpose, negotiations, previous deals, trade customs) in interpreting ambiguous or otherwise difficult provisions of the express terms when plain meaning yields no (or an unwelcome) answer. It might be argued that only the latter process truly involves interpretation. But the concept of interpretation is difficult to confine in this manner. Kent Greenawalt writes that: 'Lawyers often regard whatever factors figure in a court's final decision about how to treat a particular text as involving interpretation.'[46] Contextual interpretation may give scope for contractual interference by bypassing the safeguards presented by more rigid doctrinal techniques, such as rectification of mistakes.[47] Courts in particular display the tendency to overlap the process of contextual interpretation with more established doctrines that can rewrite the parties' obligations. This is explored further below.

Contractual controversies

The ways in which contractual interpretation is controversial will be explored during the course of the book, but some initial points

---

45 Op. cit., Schauer, p 212.
46 Greenawalt, K., 'A Pluralist Approach to Interpretation: Wills and Contracts' (2005) 42 *San Diego LR* 533, 547. Hereafter 'Pluralist'.
47 McMeel, G., 'Interpretation and Mistake in Contract Law: "The Fox Knows Many Things . . ." ' [2006] *Lloyd's MCLQ* 49, pp 52–3. On the usefulness of 'construction' in evading contract law rules see P.S. Atiyah, 'Judicial Techniques and Contract Law' in *Essays on Contract*, 1988, Oxford: OUP, 267.

will be made now. Controversies exist at a low level, over the interpretations of contracts that are actually adopted – the *Investors* decision itself contained a dissenting judgment from Lord Lloyd.[48] It is a feature of interpretations that they are generally disputed. These disputes are not always the result of the application of different interpretative strategies by the 'contextualist' as opposed to the 'literalist' judge. As Sir Thomas Bingham observed in *Arbuthnott v Fagan*, most resolutions of interpretation issues are 'neither uncompromisingly literal nor unswervingly purposive'.[49] Judges may broadly agree with the contextual approach but differ over the interpretative question that needs answering, or over the kind of materials that are relevant to 'contextual interpretation', such as prior negotiations, witness or expert evidence, or about what constitutes an 'absurd result' that justifies departure from plain meaning. This may reflect a more basic disagreement about how much freedom the parties should enjoy in framing their obligations, about the role of the documents in the agreement, and the permissible level of judicial interference in the bargain. On an even deeper level there may be disagreement about contract law's normative framework – whether its foundation ethic is based on individualism or co-operation or some mix of the two.[50] The shift to contextualism has not resolved all the problems to which contractual interpretation gives rise, and in many ways contextualism has increased the capacity for dispute, as judges disagree over what context is, what kind of contextual material is relevant and what its effect may be. It is not clear that there is a unified position between courts, parties and scholars on the subject of how 'contextual interpretation' is to be undertaken. This is partly related to the fluid and endlessly disputed nature of 'interpretation'. The difficulties in relation to this concept have prompted some to argue that the whole process of examining the nature of interpretation is distracting, since the debates are 'ultimately insoluble, because the fact that our system requires unaccountable persons to make binding legal decisions will forever remain in tension with our commitment to democracy and the rule of law'.[51]

---

48 [1998] 1 All ER 98 at p. 100.
49 *The Times*, 20 October 1993.
50 Brownsword, R., 'After *Investors*: Interpretation, Expectation and the Implicit Dimension of the "New Contextualism"' in *Implicit Dimensions*, p 103 at 124ff.
51 Op. cit., McGowan, M., 'Against Interpretation', 712.

This lack of consensus should come as no surprise since the debate over how contracts should be interpreted can be seen as part of an ongoing wider debate concerning the role of contract law in regulating the agreements that people make. The latter half of the twentieth century saw the breakdown of the classical doctrinal contract law rules in favour of the development of more flexible standards.[52] This breakdown can be traced through a number of well-known developments: the rise of the consumer as a contracting force, with attendant concerns over procedural and substantive fairness in contract law; the rise of the standard form contract and increased statutory interference in the contents of the 'bargain'; the expansion of tort law into areas regarded as the traditional preserve of contract doctrine, most notably economic loss; the weakening commitment to doctrines such as consideration and privity of contract, and the rise of estoppel; increasing European intervention in domestic contract law. The shift to contextual interpretation could be regarded as part of this general breakdown. While the social and contextual aspects of contracting are undeniable, how the law should respond (and whether judges can) to the information generated by an appreciation of the contexts of transactions is disputed. These disputes are often played out in cases concerning how contracts should be interpreted. Nevertheless, it would be misleading to assert that the movements are all one-way, since there are decisions of courts that illustrate that the rigid doctrinal structure still exercises considerable influence, especially in the lower courts where the bulk of contract litigation takes place. There is still the tendency to view 'reasonable expectations' as generated in part, if not wholly, by the legal framework of documents and rules.[53] This is sometimes manifest in the commitment to plain meaning and objective intention in interpretation. Debates over contract interpretation can thus be seen as part of a wider pattern of anxieties relating to the 'transformation' of the law of contract.[54]

---

52 See, generally, Brownsword, R., *Contract Law: Themes for the Twenty-First Century*, 2nd edn, 2006, Oxford: OUP, chs 5 and 7.

53 Mitchell, C., 'Leading a Life of its Own? The Roles of Reasonable Expectation in Contract Law' (2003) 23 *OJLS* 639, at 649–54.

54 Collins, H., *The Law of Contract*, 4th edn, 2003, London: Lexis Nexis, ch 2; Adams, J. and Brownsword, R., *Understanding Contract Law*, 4th edn, 2004, London: Sweet and Maxwell, ch 9.

Interpretation and contractual power

One might justify examining the subject of contractual interpretation by simply asserting that it is a matter of practical importance
to lawyers and their clients. But there is another more general reason for subjecting contractual interpretation to closer scrutiny. The
interpretative method courts use is arguably a barometer of judicial
attitudes towards contractual agreements more generally. Although
it is doubtful how far the common law was ever committed to literal
interpretation and enforcement of contracts according to their plain
meaning, the *perception* that it was committed to this kind of formalism at least allowed that it was consistent with particular values
that contract law sought to uphold – certainty and predictability in
enforcement of the rules, giving effect to the objective intentions of
the parties and minimalising interference in the bargain. The rules
thus kept faith with the philosophy that contractual obligations
were, fundamentally, self-imposed and voluntary. The court's role
was to enforce the agreement the parties had made, not to create and
substitute a new one. Lord Goff wrote, extrajudicially:

> In commercial transactions the duty of the court is simply to
> give effect to the contract, and not to dictate to the parties what
> the court thinks they ought to have agreed, or what a person
> (reasonable or otherwise) might have agreed if he had read
> the contract and addressed his mind to the problem, which, in
> the outcome, has arisen.[55]

One needs look no further than the speech of Lord Bingham in *The
Starsin*, to see how influential these values remain.[56] Through the
rhetoric at least, the courts concede that while contractual interpretation is about meaning, it is also an issue about power – more specifically, the balance of power and authority between the interpreter
(judge) and the creators of the thing being interpreted (the parties).
Issues about power and authority pervade theories of interpretation
generally. Such theories often divide along the lines of whom, or
what, is at the centre of the search for meaning. There is the abstract

---

55 Lord Goff, 'Commercial Contracts and the Commercial Court', [1984] *Lloyd's
    MCLQ* 382, 391. See, also, Mance LJ in *Sinochem International Oil v Mobil* [2000]
    1 Lloyd's Rep 339, at [29].
56 *Homburg Houtimport BV v Agrosin Private Ltd and others (The Starsin)* [2003]
    UKHL 12, [2003] 2 All ER 785 [9–13].

'text' or communication itself, there is the speaker/author who makes the utterance/creates the text and there is the hearer/reader/ interpreter who receives it. Thus one main conflict is between 'textualists' and 'intentionalists'.[57] Textualism demands that it is the text only that matters. Interpretation is not the search for the intentions of the author of the text, but is a search for what the words of the text *literally* mean. For intentionalists, author's intent can be the only relevant meaning, however difficult it may be practically to find the author's intention. For some intentionalists, 'interpretation' is precisely the task of deriving intention. If a person claims to be searching for something else, they are not engaged in interpretation.[58]

In relation to law, the issue of 'who or what counts' in interpretation is more familiar in debates about statutory interpretation. Here, it is a matter of controversy whether interpreters should seek to give effect to the intentions of the creators of legislation or some other group, or the plain words of the text, or some other abstract value or policy, in interpreting statutes. If intention is taken to be the guide, there is further dispute about what materials, beyond the statutory text, are relevant to accessing that intention.[59] The underlying concerns over political legitimacy and the judicial function are of course much more significant in relation to legislation than contracts – no great issues of constitutional principle turn on how contracts are interpreted. But while the stakes in contractual interpretation are lower, since the interpretation the courts finally adopt only affects the parties to the contract,[60] contracts raise similar issues about power, especially given the number of people that may be involved in both creating and interpreting the agreement (the parties, lawyers, third parties, judges). The modern approach to contractual interpretation is worth examining to discover what it reveals about current judicial attitudes towards contract law and, in particular, attitudes concerning the balance of power between the parties, judges and others.

---

57 Nelson, C., 'What is Textualism?' (2005) 91 *Virginia LR* 347, 351.
58 Fish, S., 'There is no Textualist Position' (2005) 42 *San Diego LR* 629, 635.
59 See discussion in Vogenauer, S., 'A Retreat from *Pepper v Hart*? A Reply to Lord Steyn' (2005) 25 *OJLS* 629.
60 Bowers, J.W., 'Murphy's Law and The Elementary Theory of Contract Interpretation: A Response to Schwartz and Scott' (2005) 57 *Rutgers L R* 587, n 94.

The range of interpretative problems

Even if we confine our examination to 'textual problems' of language or communication failure in contracts, there is a wide range of possible interpretation disputes. Perhaps the most common and obvious interpretation problem is simply lack of clarity in the terms due to defects of draftsmanship. This was the root of the problem in the *Investors* decision itself. In the words of Lord Lloyd, the problem 'arises not from any obscurity of the language (the meaning is, I think, tolerably clear) but from slovenly drafting'.[61] The facts were that a group of investors had compensation claims against a building society after suffering losses from being mis-sold 'home income plans' by financial advisers and the society. The claims included, *inter alia*, common law negligence, misrepresentation and rescission of mortgages. The Investors Compensation Scheme Ltd (ICS) had been set up to provide a fund from which the investors could recoup some of their losses. In return for making a claim on the fund, the investors were required to assign some of their legal claims against the society to ICS. The interpretation issue related to which claims had been assigned and which retained by the investors. This depended upon the construction placed on a provision in the claim form that the investors were required to sign. The provision maintained that the investors retained:

> Any claim (whether sounding in rescission for undue influence or otherwise) that you have or may have against the West Bromwich Building Society in which you claim an abatement of sums which you would otherwise have to repay to that Society in respect of sums borrowed by you from that Society in connection with the transaction and dealings giving rise to the claim (including interest on any such sums).

The issue was whether the investors retained 'any claim' against the building society in which they sought an abatement (reduction) in the amount due under a mortgage loan, or whether 'any claim' should be limited to a claim for abatement arising only from rescission. The latter involved rearranging the parenthesis so that the term was interpreted to read 'Any claim sounding in rescission (whether for undue influence or otherwise) that you have ... etc.,'. The natural meaning, adopted in the Court of Appeal, tended to suggest the former construction. But in the House of Lords, Lord Hoffmann (with whom three other law lords agreed) said that such an interpretation led to an absurd result. Lord Hoffmann conceded that the court was involved in making a choice between 'unnatural meanings' of the provision,[62] but said the context suggested that the investors retained claims in rescission only. The controversial issue here related to what was a 'ridiculous result' in circumstances where the contextual evidence provided little conclusive guidance one way or the other as to what was intended.

Drafting errors can occur because of limitations in the skills of the drafter or from errors of transcription. Courts are content to interpolate words in the latter circumstances provided 'it is clear both that words have been omitted and what those omitted words were'.[63] Other interpretation problems relate to unforeseen and unanticipated events, which lead the court to doubt that the contract expresses what the parties intended,[64] or mistakes and inconsistencies within the terms of the agreement.[65] In some cases, identifying the parties to the contract has been treated as a matter of interpretation of the contractual documents.[66] Context may of course generate inconsistency when the natural meaning of the words seems clear and easily applicable to the case at hand, but appears to contradict contextual material, such as the customs of the trade.[67] Plain meanings may be regarded as giving rise to unreasonable or 'uncommercial' results, which necessitates some other interpretative approach. Some of these cases, and the difficulties they raise, are explored in greater detail in the next chapter.

Many interpretative difficulties arise not from problems of drafting and ambiguous word meaning, but the over- and under-inclusiveness of rules and contract terms.[68] An illustration is provided by the

---

62 Ibid., p 116.
63 Per Lord Bingham, *The Starsin*, [23].
64 For example, *Bank of Credit and Commerce International SA (in liquidation) v Ali* [2001] UKHL 8, [2001] 2 WLR 735.
65 For example, *Mannai Investment Co Ltd v Eagle Star Life Assurance Co Ltd* [1997] 3 All ER 352.
66 *Shogun Finance Ltd v Hudson* [2003] UKHL 62, [2003] 3 WLR 1371; *The Starsin* [2003] UKHL 12, [2003] 2 All ER 785.
67 *Exxonmobil Sales and Supply Corporation v Texaco Ltd: The Helene Knutsen* [2003] EWHC 1964, [2003] 2 Lloyd's Rep 686.
68 Op. cit., Schauer, p 135.

Court of Appeal decision in *Hayward v Norwich Union Insurance*.[69]
In this case the claimant's car had been stolen while he was paying
for petrol in a service station kiosk. The car had been left unlocked
with the keys in the ignition. The car was fitted with an immobiliser,
which was armed, but the thief had managed to override its operation. The defendant insurance company refused to indemnify the
claimant for the theft, since the insurance policy excluded 'Loss or
damage arising from theft whilst the ignition keys of your car have
been left in or on the car'. On the face of it, the claimant had certainly left his keys in the car. However, the first instance judge
thought there was an ambiguity and interpreted the exception as
meaning the car had been 'left unattended'. He accepted the claimant's argument that although the keys had been left in the car, the car
had not been left unattended. The Court of Appeal overturned this,
adopting the plain meaning of the words. But Peter Gibson LJ did
note how changing the factual situation – or context – could change
the interpretation of 'left in the car':

> . . . the driver leaves the key in the ignition while he fills up and
> pays for petrol at a time when there is a passenger in the car.
> Whether the keys have been left in those circumstances must, in
> my view, depend on the circumstances. If the passenger is an
> adult in whose charge the keys have been left so that such person
> stands in for the driver, then on the plain and ordinary meaning
> of the words of the Exception the keys have not been left in the
> car. But if the passenger is, for example, a small child, then the
> presence of the passenger will not prevent the keys from having
> been left. A second situation is where there is a hijacking, the
> driver for example being pulled out of the car while the keys are
> in the ignition. In my judgment such duress prevents the keys
> from being 'left' in the car.[70]

Of course the plain meaning of the words, 'left in the car', does not
change and we might maintain that there is no linguistic difficulty
here. Rather, the problem is that the changing factual context leaves
room for doubt whether the exception ought to be applied to deprive
the claimant of insurance cover. It is the familiar problem of whether
the literal meaning should be departed from in favour of examining

---

69 [2001] EWCA Civ 243, *The Times* 8 March 2001.
70 At para [28].

the purposes of the provision to decide whether the situation falls within the scope of the provision or not. One might therefore categorise this problem as not concerned with interpretation at all, but with the 'applicability of rules to facts'.[71] Similarly, a text may have a plain meaning which yields an *unwelcome* answer rather than no answer, that is, an answer that would seem to run counter to some value or policy that contract law supposedly supports. The process required to avoid this unwelcome result may be described as involving interpretation, even when the meaning of the text is clear. In truth, it might be better categorised as some other task, such as the application of policy to a rule, or reading the rule in the light of a principle, rather than interpretation. While it is clear that drawing such distinctions between these different tasks is theoretically possible, in practice it is much harder to distinguish 'interpretation' from other activities. Certainly the courts seldom adopt such rigid distinctions, as the next section demonstrates.

Interpretation or something else?

Interpretation and implication

Courts are often required to fill gaps in an agreement. When a court implies terms in an agreement is it correct to say they are interpreting it?[72] Implication is usually regarded as a process of adding terms rather than seeking to understand terms already written. In this way implication appears to be more of a creative process than interpretation, although the courts frequently deny that implication creates obligations for the parties, rather the court draws out what is implicit in the agreement. In relation to terms implied in fact into specific contracts – those that 'go without saying' or are necessary to make the contract work – it would seem genuine to describe the process as one of 'interpretation' of the agreement.[73] Most of these

71 Simpson, A.W.B., 'The *Ratio Decidendi* of a Case and the Doctrine of Binding Precedent', in A.G. Guest (ed.), *Oxford Essays in Jurisprudence*, 1961, Oxford: OUP, p 158.

72 Several scholars have considered the relationship between implication and interpretation. Recent contributions include, op. cit., Smith, S., ch 8; Kramer, A., 'Implication in Fact as an Instance of Contractual Interpretation' (2004) 63 *CLJ* 384 (hereafter 'Implication in Fact'); op. cit., Collins, 'Committed Contextualism', pp 200–1.

73 Op. cit., Smith, S., p 280.

sorts of gaps can be filled by a process of pragmatic inference ('reading between the lines' or 'what goes without saying') on the basis of what has been expressly stated, even if not actually thought of or intended by the parties.[74] This is clearly an interpretative technique. Terms implied by law into all contracts of a general type, for example the implied term of trust and confidence in employment contracts,[75] may be more difficult to justify as coming within the range of interpretation. Such terms usually have some normative or policy foundation. For many scholars the process of implying terms is regarded as part of the wider technique of interpretation. Thus Sir Kim Lewison devotes an entire chapter to implied terms in his work, *The Interpretation of Contracts*.[76] This is not uncontroversial however. Ewan McKendrick, in his review of Lewison, suggests that the processes of implication and interpretation of terms are 'analytically distinct'.[77] McKendrick does not state how the processes are analytically distinct, but the difference between 'gap filling' as opposed to understanding the text is the most likely explanation.

Judges too, differ over this question. Lord Hoffmann clearly regards the process of implication as part of interpretation. Writing extrajudicially he stated, 'the implication of a term into a contract is an exercise in interpretation like any other ... the only difference is that when we imply a term, we are engaged in interpreting the meaning of the contract as a whole'.[78] Lord Steyn would seem to regard the distinction as more problematic. In *Equitable Life Assurance Society v Hyman*, he said the process of interpretation 'assign[s] to the language of the text the most appropriate meaning which the words can legitimately bear.'[79] Implied terms, on the other hand 'operate as ad hoc gap fillers'. The distinction seems to turn on the difference between understanding *the language of the text* and circumstances where there is no text: if there is no text, there can be nothing to interpret. But this only seems to reiterate the obvious difference between express terms and implied terms. If we instead ask *how express terms are to be understood* and compare this with

74 Op. cit., Kramer, p 385ff; op. cit., Smith, p 300.
75 *Malik and Mahmud v Bank of Credit and Commerce International SA (in liq)* [1997] 3 All ER 1.
76 3rd edn, 2004, London: Sweet and Maxwell, ch 6.
77 [2005] *LQR* 158, 159.
78 'Intolerable Wrestle', op. cit., p 662.
79 [2002] 1 AC 408, p 458.

how terms are to be implied, the distinction disappears. So, when Lord Steyn considers the justification for implication he writes that 'if a term is to be implied, it could only be a term implied from the language of [a contract term] read in its particular commercial setting.' He continues, 'Such a term may be imputed to parties: it is not critically dependent on proof of an actual intention of the parties. The process "is one of construction of the agreement as a whole in its commercial setting" '.[80] This suggests implication is part of a wider process of interpretation: the method for deriving an implied term from the language is the same as that demanded in contextual interpretation of the language. In addition, in *Sirius International Insurance Company v FAI General Insurance Ltd*, Lord Steyn, after undertaking the contextual interpretation of a term to ascertain its meaning, remarked, 'If it were necessary I would reach this conclusion on the basis of a constructional implication.'[81] Although he does not explain 'constructional implication', this suggests interpretation and implication are very closely connected, if not indistinguishable.

Some scholars also support the connection between interpretation and implication. For Adam Kramer, both implication and contextual interpretation can be regarded as part of the same overall process – that of 'supplementation' of the contract. The difference between them relates to the kind of information that is sought to be added by each process, or 'what it was reasonable to understand as going without saying'.[82] Contextual interpretation has a lower justificatory threshold – courts can supplement the information provided by the contract with what is reasonable to infer from the context. This process is suitable for the kind of information that is yielded from 'reading between the lines'. Implication, on the other hand, is required when the added material is much less likely to go without saying and so cannot be inferred. Adding terms in these circumstances requires a higher justificatory threshold than supplementation through contextual interpretation – the requirements of the intentions of the parties and necessity must be satisfied.[83] Collins has also conceded that implying terms is 'closely related to the

---

80 Ibid. at p 459, quoting Lord Hoffmann in *Banque Bruxelles Lambert SA v Eagle Star Insurance Co. Ltd* [1997] AC 191, 212.
81 [2004] UKHL 54, at [25].
82 Op. cit., Kramer, p 385.
83 Op. cit., Kramer, p 401.

activity of interpretation'.[84] But he has also pointed out that they are justified on slightly different grounds: interpretation is based on a thorough objectivist approach ('what a reasonable promisee would have understood by the text'[85]), whereas implication is based on the common intention of the parties in relation to the commercial purposes of their agreement.[86] While this distinction might be notionally correct – implied terms, at least in fact, are subject to the test of necessity rather than reasonableness[87] – other ways of expressing the test in terms of 'officious bystander' and business efficacy seem to suggest a more reasonableness-based and contextual approach that may be in practice indistinguishable from interpretation. At the very least, implication is a technique for giving effect to a chosen interpretation of the agreement.

Interpretation and construction

There are of course many other techniques by which the court can give effect to particular interpretations, in addition to the implication of terms. Rectification and the use of collateral contracts are further examples. Sometimes use of these techniques is referred to as contractual 'construction'. Most judges use the terms 'construction' and 'interpretation' interchangeably,[88] but some commentators have regarded these as qualitatively different processes. Interpretation may be regarded as being limited to fixing on the meaning of the express words in the agreement in instances of ambiguity or vagueness, whereas 'construction' describes the next step of determining the parties' obligations based on that interpretation. Elizabeth Peden, for example, draws the following distinction: ' "Interpretation" describes the process whereby courts determine the meaning of words, and "construction" describes the process of determining their legal effect.'[89] Interpretation may therefore be part of construction,

---

84 Collins, 'Committed Contextualism', p 200.
85 Ibid., Collins, p 201.
86 Ibid., Collins.
87 *Liverpool City Council v Irwin* [1977] AC 239.
88 See, for example the judgment of Lord Steyn in *Deutsche Genossenschaftsbank v Burnhope* [1995] 1 WLR 1580.
89 Peden, E., ' "Cooperation" in English Contract Law: to Construe or Imply?' (2000) 9 *JCL Lexis* 1, 4. See, also, Farnsworth, E.A., ' "Meaning" in the Law of Contracts' (1967) 76 *Yale LJ* 939–40, 965; Patterson, E.W., 'The Interpretation and Construction of Contracts' (1964) 64 *Columbia LR* 833, 835.

the latter also encompassing the application of policies, principles, implied terms and so on. This might be required if the linguistic approach of interpretation yields no answer.[90] In this way, construction can be regarded as the process of attempting to understand the entire contractual relationship, rather than the narrower process of fixing on the meaning of the communicative language.

Are there any advantages in conceiving interpretation, implication and construction as qualitatively different tasks? One advantage might be greater conceptual and terminological neatness. It would allow us to form a clearer distinction between what is a genuine interpretative dispute concerning language and word-meaning, what is an imposition of an additional obligation and what is an application of policy.[91] This in turn may make judges more appreciative of the precise grounds and arguments upon which they have reached their decision. As a matter of descriptive accuracy, however, the distinctions fail. For example, courts rarely make any attempt to distinguish construction and interpretation. Indeed, to attempt to do so would be to try and impose some order on a concept that almost wholly resists it. Lord Hoffmann's own formulation of contextual interpretation, in particular the approach of taking the background to include anything the reasonable man regards as relevant, would seem to be antithetical to such a rigid division of tasks. As Lord Phillips in *Shogun Finance v Hudson* observed, 'the task of ascertaining whether the parties have reached agreement as to the terms of a contract largely overlaps with the task of ascertaining what it is that the parties have agreed'.[92] The interpretation exercise is precisely directed towards the meaning of the contractual relationship as a whole and with contractual *purposes*. Contracts aim to bring about some state of affairs, for parties to voluntarily curtail their freedom of action by undertaking legal obligations towards others, and it is hard to conclude that understanding these complexities, and understanding what the parties have agreed, can be reduced to a matter of only the interpretation of language. The idea of interpretation as a very discrete activity, separate from other sorts of activity, is difficult to sustain.

90 Ibid., Patterson, E.W., p 835.
91 Ibid., Patterson, E.W., p 837.
92 [2003] UKHL 62, [2003] 3 WLR 1371 at [124].

Why do contractual interpretation disputes exist?

Some of the reasons why interpretation disputes exist have already been explored. In relation to the contractual documents, interpretation problems arise from the indeterminacy of language, or its open texture. A more cynical answer to why interpretation disputes exist is that it often serves one party's interests to demonstrate vagueness or uncertainty in order to evade or impose liability for something. As Neil MacCormick writes, 'Almost any rule can prove to be ambiguous or unclear in relation to some disputed or disputable context of litigation'.[93] What goes for a rule also goes for a contract term. A dispute revolving around interpretation is very easy to generate in a practice heavily reliant on documents. Parties want the interpretation dispute resolved not because they want to know what the contract means, but because the interpretation is instrumental to the imposition of legal liability. Many interpretation disputes arise because of the generation of uncertainty by one of the parties, or the factual situation, rather than the inadvertence or errors on the part of the drafter. Contextual material may be crucial here in raising doubts about whether the natural meaning of the contract can accord with what the parties intended. The issue then becomes whether extrinsic evidence should be adduced for the purposes of *demonstrating* the existence of ambiguity, rather than *resolving* an ambiguity that appears on the face of the documents. Lord Hoffmann's restatement of the principles of interpretation appears to encourage the former kind of enquiry, as will be seen.

Some reasons for interpretation disputes are related to human error in drafting clauses that do not accurately represent the parties' intentions. Alternatively, some clauses will be left deliberately vague precisely for determination at a later date. Other reasons relate to the circumstances and costs of drafting more complete 'interpretation-proof' terms. Drafting a contract that covers all future eventualities is an impossibility, and contracts will always be incomplete or vague in some sense. Parties must balance the risk of an occurrence with the costs of providing for it in the formation stage of an agreement. In relation to the inevitable social context of making agreements, achieving an accurate and exhaustive record of obligations may be

---

93 MacCormick, N., *Legal Reasoning and Legal Theory*, revised edn, 1994, Oxford: OUP, pp 65–6.

antithetical to many business relationships that rely on trust and co-operation.[94] Written contracts may be regarded as unnecessary or positively unhelpful to the business relationship. How these distinctions between the social and legal frameworks of contract impinge on contractual interpretation is considered further in Chapter 4. Another problem may simply be that of haste in entering into the agreement.[95] In most contracts the main subject matter and terms (price, delivery arrangements) will be known, but subsidiary terms will not. Sometimes an interpretation problem may be taken to arise because applying the contract as written is unwelcome for some reason, usually because it appears contrary to the contractual purposes, or contravenes some vaguely defined 'policy'. It is difficult to generalise further, given the difficulty of clearly distinguishing the precise ambit of interpretation, and the endless possibilities for dispute posed by commercial relationships.

Conclusion

This chapter has sought to demonstrate the fluid and flexible nature of ideas of contract, context and interpretation. The pervasiveness of interpretation and the difficulties of adequately defining a 'contract' mean contractual interpretation is not a process that is easily limited to issues concerning the meaning of words in contractual documents. It matters, then, how the courts carry out the interpretative task. The reach of interpretation, coupled with the expansion in contractual information that contextualism appears to demand, potentially provides considerable leeway for judicial interference in the bargain. Having noted the difficulties of reining in the concept of interpretation, the next task is to examine more fully what contextual interpretation means, what it requires in commercial contract disputes and how it can be constrained.

---

94 See, for example, the facts of *Baird Textile Holdings Ltd v Marks & Spencer plc* [2001] EWCA Civ 274, where a 30-year business relationship was sustained by trust and co-operation rather than contract.

95 For a judicial appreciation of the circumstances in which agreements come into being, and the haste with which dealings are concluded, see, op. cit., Lord Walker in *Sirius v FAI*, paras [30–33].

Chapter 2

Contract interpretation and the rise of contextualism

In the last chapter the general nature of interpretation in contract law was examined. Areas of dispute, such as whether plain meaning of texts is possible and how the notion of 'a contract' should be understood, were noted. This chapter will examine more fully the approaches the courts adopt when interpreting contracts. The 'rules of construction' that the courts have traditionally applied will be briefly considered, before examining Lord Hoffmann's restatement of the principles of contractual interpretation. Since Lord Hoffmann stated that the 'intellectual baggage' of legal interpretation has been discarded, it may be that the technical rules of construction are no longer relevant. Nevertheless, elements of that baggage will be briefly examined here to get an indication of the significance and direction of Lord Hoffmann's change.[1] The more significant features of Lord Hoffmann's speech will be drawn out and explained. The difficulties with contextual interpretation will then be explored in Chapter 3.

Principles of interpretation

The first point to note is that interpretation of the agreement (at least in the context of litigation) is regarded as a role for the court, not the parties. Interpretation is question of law, not fact.[2] Since almost every interpretation problem is unique, precedents have a limited role in settling interpretative disputes. In *Bank of Credit and Commerce*

---

1 For more in-depth coverage of the interpretation rules see Lewison, K., *The Interpretation of Contracts*, 3rd edn, 2004, London: Sweet and Maxwell.
2 See Lord Diplock, *Bahamas International Trust Co Ltd v Threadgold* [1974] 1 WLR 1514, quoted in ibid., Lewison, p 96.

International SA (in liquidation) v Ali Lord Hoffmann remarked, 'If interpretation is the quest to discover what a reasonable man would have understood specific parties to have meant by the use of specific language in a specific situation at a specific time and place, how can that be affected by authority?'[3] Nevertheless, it would not be true to say that precedent plays no role. The law may seek some uniformity in the basic principles of interpretation that are applied, rather than any uniformity in result. However difficult it is to demonstrate that one has reached the 'correct' substantive interpretation on the facts, one can at least demonstrate that one has applied the 'correct' interpretative methods. It is clear that Lord Hoffmann's statement is now the authoritative dictum on how contractual interpretation should be undertaken. Precedent may also have a larger role where a particular phrase is common in contracts in a particular industry or sector. Generally speaking, if a particular interpretation of a well-used contract term (or rule) has stood for a long time then that may make the courts reluctant to overturn it, even if they could be persuaded that the interpretation might be incorrect. This argument may be particularly forceful in commercial matters, where certainty is thought to be a value. A long-standing ruling on interpretation would have to be consistently working unsatisfactorily in the marketplace, or be producing absurd results, before the House of Lords would consider overturning it – a high threshold of justification for interference.[4] Nevertheless, precedents dealing with points of interpretation are more easily distinguishable than most. This gives the courts a certain amount of latitude in an interpretation case, enabling them to seek the result that appears to be 'commercially sensible', in all the circumstances.

Another broad principle is that interpretation is the search for the objective intentions of the parties. Staughton LJ has written extra-judicially that, 'Rule One is that the task of the judge when interpreting a written contract is to find the intention of the parties. In so far as one can be sure of anything these days, that proposition is unchallenged'.[5] The search for author's intent is at the centre of many

---

3   Hereafter, *BCCI v Ali* [2001] UKHL 8, [2001] 2 WLR 735, para [51].

4   *Jindal Iron and Steel Co Limited v Islamic Solidarity Shipping Company Jordan Inc* [2004] UKHL 49, [2005] 1 All ER 175, paras [15–16]. For a recent overturning of an established interpretation of a provision see *National Westminster Bank plc v Spectrum Plus Ltd* [2005] UKHL 41, [2005] 2 AC 680.

5   Staughton, Sir C., 'How do the Courts Interpret Commercial Contracts?' (1999) 58 *CLJ* 303, p 304.

general approaches to interpretation, but it raises numerous well-known difficulties in relation to contracts, some of which were discussed in Chapter 1. Contracting parties may not be the authors of the document; there may be multiple authors, parties may be unaware of the content of the 'small print', parties may lack any intentions in relation to the specific problem that has arisen and so on. Given these difficulties, there is room for some doubt as to how far contract interpretation is concerned, both practically and theoretically, with uncovering the parties' intentions. The role of intention in contract interpretation is discussed further, below. For now, it can be noted that since contractual interpretation is concerned with intent only to the extent that it can be objectively established, this tends to favour the written contractual text as the thing to be interpreted. It is the intentions revealed by the language which are important, not the subjective intentions of each contracting party. So, for example, Lord Steyn in *Deutsche Genossenschaftsbank v Burnhope* said that:

> It is true the objective of the construction of a contract is to give effect to the intention of the parties. But our law of construction is based on an objective theory. The methodology is not to probe the real intentions of the parties but to ascertain the contextual meaning of the relevant contractual language. Intention is determined by reference to expressed rather than actual intention. The question therefore resolves itself in a search for the meaning of language in its contractual setting.[6]

Although courts may say that their purpose in interpretation is to uncover the intentions of the parties, the commitment to objectivity and the language of the documents indicate that their approach is more textualist than intentionalist. The concentration on text and objectivity is no doubt connected to a contract judge's perception of their role in the dispute – to bring out the meaning of the agreement rather than impose an outcome – and the desire to demonstrate some constraints in an activity where they readily admit that precedent plays a limited role. This would also help to explain the belief in the importance of plain meaning. The commitment to the written documents and the idea of plain meaning is not without cost, however. Joseph Perillo argues that:

---

6 *Deutsche Genossenschaftsbank v Burnhope* [1995] 1 WLR 1580, p 1587.

A highly objective vantage point [e.g. a plain meaning rule]
may be rather remote from the perspectives of the parties and
may produce an interpretation that conforms to the intention of
neither party . . . This perspective subordinates the parties'
intentions of the intrinsic meaning of words.[7]

The textualist approach to interpretation is also bolstered by the
operation of the parol evidence rule, which accords primacy to complete contractual documents, where they exist. The rule is that 'where
a contract has been reduced to writing, neither party can rely on
extrinsic evidence of terms alleged to have been agreed, i.e., on evidence not contained in the document'.[8] Like the requirement of consideration, the parol evidence rule is subject to so many exceptions
that it rarely causes injustice or practical problems.[9] Extrinsic evidence may be allowed, for example if the contract is not complete, or
to show a mistake or misrepresentation, or the existence of a collateral contract, or if the contract contains specialist terms that
need interpretation or explanation (in relation to trade customs, for
example).[10] The issue of contractual 'completeness' is said to be a
function of the objective intentions of the parties, but it may depend
more on whether the available documents appear to be complete
to the adjudicator. The documents may look complete if they are
'long and detailed, or at least contain unconditional language, cover
many contingencies, or at least the most important contingencies,
and contain a clause, such as a merger [entire agreement] clause,
which says that the contract is complete.'[11] But even this may not be
conclusive. The inference about the intentions of the parties if the
documents look complete is fairly easily overturned. For some commentators the legal record will always lack completeness, since it
may bear little relation to the 'reasonable expectations' of the parties

---

7 Perillo, J., 'The Origins of the Objective Theory of Contract Formation and Interpretation' (2000) 68 *Fordham LR* 427, 431. Hereafter, 'Objective Theory'.
8 Treitel, G., *The Law of Contract*, 11th edn, 2003, London: Sweet and Maxwell,
   p 192.
9 Law Commission, *Law of Contract: The Parol Evidence Rule*, No 154, 1986,
   para 2.7; McKendrick, E., *Contract Law: Text, Cases and Materials*, 2nd edn,
   2005, Oxford: OUP, p 340. *Contra*, see ibid., Treitel, pp 193–5 and Collins,
   Regulating Contracts, pp 159–60.
10 Ibid., Treitel, pp 193–201.
11 Posner, E., 'The Parol Evidence Rule, the Plain Meaning Rule and the Principles
   of Contractual Interpretation' (1998) 146 *Univ Pennsylvania LR* 533, 535.

that arise and are given substance by other aspects of the business relationship.[12]

Despite the various mechanisms for extending the court's reach to evidence outside the four corners of the document, for practical, historical and normative reasons, contract law has generally taken the view that the signed contractual text, where available, is authoritative. Thus Lord Steyn writes, '[t]he mandated point of departure must be the text itself. The primacy of the text is the first rule of interpretation for the judge considering a point of interpretation. Extrinsic materials are therefore subordinate to the text itself'.[13] The strength of this position is well-illustrated by the recent decision of the House of Lords on mistaken identity: *Shogun Finance v Hudson*. This case raised the issue of who is a party to a hire purchase contract – the person with whom another has been dealing face to face, or the person identified in the documents? In *Shogun*, a fraudster, who was in possession of the stolen driving licence of a Mr Patel, visited a car dealer. The dealer agreed to sell him a car and the fraudster completed a standard hire-purchase agreement. This document identified Mr Patel as the debtor. The deal was approved by the finance company; the fraudster took the car away and almost immediately sold it to an innocent third party. When the fraud was discovered, the finance company sought to recover the car from the third party. They could do so only if they could establish that the debtor under the agreement was Mr Patel. If the debtor was Mr Patel, rather than the fraudster, then the contract was void and the third party would not have received good title to the car. By a 3:2 majority the House of Lords held that Mr Patel was the debtor. For Lord Hobhouse the issue of identity was a matter of the construction of the documents. The agreement was concluded in writing and since the documents identified Mr Patel as the contractor, and contained all his details, the agreement could not be with the fraudster. To say otherwise was an attempt to introduce oral evidence to contradict the written form of the agreement. His Lordship defended the parol evidence rule in robust terms. He referred to the rule as 'one of the great strengths of English commercial law' and 'one of the main reasons for the international success of English law in

12 Collins, *Regulating Contracts*, ch 6.
13 Lord Steyn, 'The Intractable Problem of the Interpretation of Legal Texts' in S. Worthington (ed.) *Commercial Law and Commercial Practice*, 2003, Oxford: Hart, 123, 125.

preference to laxer systems which do not provide the same certainty'.[14] Although the correctness of applying the parol evidence rule to a void contract is doubtful,[15] the idea that the identity of the contracting parties may be a matter of the interpretation of the text, rather than an assessment of the factual realities of what took place on the dealership's premises, speaks volumes about the primacy accorded to documents by contract law.

The reasons for the primacy accorded to written documents are partly historical. In relation to contracts under seal, the parol evidence rule was not necessary. Contracts under seal were complete documents that constituted the contract. As unsealed written documents became more common, the parol evidence rule was created to protect such documents from being undermined on the basis that they did not reflect one or other of the parties' subjective intent.[16] The Statute of Frauds 1677 also required certain contracts to be made in writing.[17] There are other practical reasons for the primacy accorded to the documents in the contractual scheme. For lawyers, documents minimise the possibility for error in recalling what was agreed (in the drafting stage lawyers will of course be anticipating, and seeking to minimise, the possibility of a dispute). Written, and signed, contracts may still have an important social function of symbolising the seriousness and implications of the undertaking as well as providing manageable evidence of what was decided.[18] Whether contracting parties read terms and conditions or not, almost everyone appreciates that signing a document entails some legal consequences.[19] Thus Lord Devlin wrote that businessmen 'like the solemnity of the contract, but do not care about its details'.[20] Indeed, the existence of the lawyer-drafted written document may

14 Per Lord Hobhouse, *Shogun Finance v Hudson* [2003] 3 WLR 1371 at 1386. Lord Walker concurred.
15 Lord Hobhouse's reference to the parol evidence rule has been criticised: 'The parol evidence rule has never before in its history been used as a tool to defeat a defence raised by a non-party to a non-contract recorded in a worthless document': McMeel, G., 'Interpretation and Mistake in Contract Law: "The Fox Knows Many Things . . ." ' [2006] *Lloyd's MCLQ* 49, p 75.
16 Perillo, 'Objective Theory', 435.
17 Smith, S., *Atiyah's Introduction to the Law of Contract*, 2005, Oxford: OUP, 94 and ibid., Perillo, 435.
18 Fuller, L., 'Consideration and Form' (1941) *Col. LR* 799, 800–3.
19 Op. cit., Smith, S., *Atiyah's Introduction*, 137–8.
20 Lord Devlin, 'The Relationship between Commercial Law and Commercial Practice', 1951, 14 *MLR* 249, 266.

constitute a 'context' in its own right. Thus Smith argues that 'The context of commercial drafting . . . is one that asks the reader to ignore the context outside of the physical document. *Why* this is the context is not strictly relevant, but the reason is undoubtedly found in the importance that commercial lawyers place on reducing opportunities for misunderstandings'.[21] Thus reliance on written documents reduces the scope for disputes about the agreement.[22] Along with the parol evidence rule, another exclusionary rule of evidence relates to prior negotiations and subsequent conduct. The prior negotiations rule excludes evidence of previous drafts of contracts, and evidence of what was said or done in negotiations, when interpreting agreements. Similarly, conduct of the parties subsequent to the agreement is not admissible in the issue of deciding what the contract means. There are several exceptions to these rules and the emerging view is that the continued exclusion of this evidence is incompatible with contextual interpretation. This issue is considered further in the next chapter.

In addition to the general principles and exclusionary rules, there are also more specific interpretation techniques, or canons of construction that a court may use. Perhaps the most widely known of these is the *contra proferentem* rule. Broadly speaking, this states that if the meaning of a term is ambiguous, the interpretation that is least favourable to the person advancing the term should be adopted.[23] The rule proved particularly effective for controlling excluding and limiting terms prior to the inception of the Unfair Contract Terms Act 1977, but it is unclear whether it will operate in the same way since Lord Hoffmann's restatement. The rule would seem to form part of the 'intellectual baggage' that Lord Hoffmann was keen to discard. In *Sinochem International Oil (London) Co Ltd v Mobil Sales and Supply Corporation*, the rule was described as one of 'last resort'.[24] Yet it is still regularly applied.[25] Other similar maxims include *ejusdem generis*: 'a general term joined with a specific one will be deemed to include only things that are like (of the same genus as) the specific

21 Smith, S., *Contract Theory*, p 276.
22 Lord Nicholls, 'My Kingdom for a Horse: The Meaning of Words' (2005) 1 *LQR* 577, 585.
23 *Houghton v Trafalgar Insurance Co Ltd* [1955] 1 QB 247.
24 Per Mance LJ, [2000] 1 Lloyd's Rep 339, at [27].
25 For a recent application of the rule see *Lexi Holdings plc v Stainforth* [2006] EWCA Civ 988.

one';[26] and *expressio unius exclusio alterius*: if specific words rather than general words are used, things of a similar kind are excluded. Finally, if there is a contradiction between printed standard terms and conditions that purport to govern the contract, and terms that the parties have written in themselves, the latter take priority.[27] This is a more widely utilised rule of interpretation. It is mirrored, for example in the Principles of European Contract Law, which place more weight on individually negotiated terms than imposed standard terms and conditions.[28]

Literalism in contracts interpretation

None of these principles of construction in themselves suggest that the English courts' approach to interpretation is unduly literal or formalistic, although the tendency towards formalism is displayed in seeking to impose rule-bound order and structure on interpretation when it is, by its nature, a more intuitive and impressionistic process. Certainly the perception is that, historically at least, English law preferred a literal approach to contract interpretation, only looking beyond the plain meaning of words in cases of ambiguity, uncertainty or absurdity. This is a difficult image for English law to abandon, particularly when it has been perceived as one of its strengths.[29] The case of *Lovell and Christmas Ltd v Wall* is often taken to be an exemplar of the literal approach. In the relevant passage, Cozens-Hardy MR states that a document should be construed, 'according to the *ordinary grammatical meaning of the words used therein*, and without reference to anything which has previously passed between the parties to it.'[30] *Lovell* was decided in 1911, but in

---

26 Patterson, E.W., 'The Interpretation and Construction of Contracts' (1964) 64 *Columbia LR* 833, 853.

27 *The Starsin*, [2003] UKHL 12, [2003] 2 All ER 785, per Lord Bingham, at [11].

28 Art. 5:104. By way of contrast, the UNIDROIT Principles of International Commercial Contracts (2004) stipulate that 'Contract terms shall be interpreted so as to give effect to all the terms rather than to deprive some of them of effect': Art. 4.5. The expectations of commercial contractors are an important consideration in relation to the latter.

29 Particularly in commercial contracts: see Steyn, Lord, 'Does Legal Formalism Hold Sway in England?' (1996) 49 *CLP* 43, p 58; Lord Irvine, 'The Law: An Engine for Trade' (2001) 64 *MLR* 333, p 334.

30 (1911) 104 LT 85, 88. The case is given in McKendrick, E., *Contract Law: Text, Cases and Materials*, 2nd edn, p 405, as an exemplar of the literal approach.

1984 Lord Goff wrote, extrajudicially, that 'English courts do not lightly depart from the literal interpretation'.[31] This commitment to literalism is disputed, however, and other judges deny that literalism has ever formed part of common law method.[32] Indeed a purely literal approach to interpretation would seem to be impossible. As with so much in interpretation, it is all a matter of degree. In *Prenn v Simmonds*, Lord Wilberforce remarked that 'The time has long passed when agreements, even those under seal, were isolated from the matrix of facts in which they were set and interpreted purely on internal linguistic considerations.'[33] Lord Wilberforce traced authority for a more liberal approach to 1877 and the judgment of Lord Blackburn in *River Wear Commissioners v Adamson*.[34] It is therefore difficult to discern a time when contracts were interpreted *solely* on the basis of 'internal linguistic considerations', and without reference to any other factors. This suggests that interpretative positions are not as polarised as some might assume, and that any claim to novelty in Lord Hoffmann's *Investors* speech is something of an overstatement. This need not concern us overmuch, since the issue of originality is not the most significant aspect of Lord Hoffmann's speech.

Lord Hoffmann's restatement

The relevant passage is reproduced here in its entirety:

> . . . I think I should preface my explanation of my reasons with some general remarks about the principles by which contractual documents are nowadays construed. I do not think that the fundamental change which has overtaken this branch of the law, particularly as a result of the speeches of Lord Wilberforce in *Prenn v Simmonds* [1971] 1 W.L.R. 1381, 1384–1386 and *Reardon Smith Line Ltd. v Yngvar Hansen-Tangen* [1976] 1 W.L.R. 989, is always sufficiently appreciated. The result has been, subject to one important exception, to assimilate the way

31 'Commercial Contracts and the Commercial Court' [1984] *Lloyd's MCLQ* 382, at 388.
32 See, for example, Lord Steyn in *Sirius v FAI* [2004] UKHL 54, [2005] 1 All ER 191 at [19]; *Mitsubishi Corp v Eastwind Transport* [2004] EWHC 2924 at [28].
33 [1971] 1 WLR 1381, pp 1383–4.
34 (1877) 2 App Cas 743.

in which such documents are interpreted by judges to the common sense principles by which any serious utterance would be interpreted in ordinary life. Almost all the old intellectual baggage of 'legal' interpretation has been discarded. The principles may be summarised as follows:

(1) Interpretation is the ascertainment of the meaning which the document would convey to a reasonable person having all the background knowledge which would reasonably have been available to the parties in the situation in which they were at the time of the contract.

(2) The background was famously referred to by Lord Wilberforce as the 'matrix of fact', but this phrase is, if anything, an understated description of what the background may include. Subject to the requirement that it should have been reasonably available to the parties and to the exception to be mentioned next, it includes absolutely anything which would have affected the way in which the language of the document would have been understood by a reasonable man.

(3) The law excludes from the admissible background the previous negotiations of the parties and their declarations of subjective intent. They are admissible only in an action for rectification. The law makes this distinction for reasons of practical policy and, in this respect only, legal interpretation differs from the way we would interpret utterances in ordinary life. The boundaries of this exception are in some respects unclear. But this is not the occasion on which to explore them.

(4) The meaning which a document (or any other utterance) would convey to a reasonable man is not the same thing as the meaning of its words. The meaning of words is a matter of dictionaries and grammars; the meaning of the document is what the parties using those words against the relevant background would reasonably have been understood to mean. The background may not merely enable the reasonable man to choose between the possible meanings of words which are ambiguous but even (as occasionally happens in ordinary life) to conclude that the parties must, for whatever reason, have used the wrong words or syntax. (see *Mannai Investments Co Ltd v Eagle Star Life Assurance Co. Ltd.* [1997] 2 WLR 945).

(5) The 'rule' that words should be given their 'natural and ordinary meaning' reflects the common sense proposition that

we do not easily accept that people have made linguistic mistakes, particularly in formal documents. On the other hand, if one would nevertheless conclude from the background that something must have gone wrong with the language, the law does not require judges to attribute to the parties an intention which they plainly could not have had. Lord Diplock made this point more vigorously when he said in *The Antaios Compania Neviera SA v Salen Rederierna AB* [1985] 1 AC 191, 201: '. . . if detailed semantic and syntactical analysis of words in a commercial contract is going to lead to a conclusion that flouts business commonsense, it must be made to yield to business commonsense.'[35]

What is interpretation and when is it required?

What important factors should be drawn out of this passage? The first issue relates to Lord Hoffmann's ideas on interpretative method. He remarks that the full implications of the principles developed by Lord Wilberforce have not been 'sufficiently appreciated'. Arguably, the insufficiently appreciated factor is that contextual interpretation is the only method at work. Inquiries into context, 'factual matrix' or 'background' are not second-level approaches when the first-level inquiry into plain meaning yields no answer. For Lord Hoffmann, there is *no such thing* as purely textual, literal or plain meaning interpretation: all instances of fixing on contractual meaning must involve contextual interpretation *at some level*. Some judges have certainly understood Lord Hoffmann to be making this claim. Lord Steyn in *R (on the application of Westminster City Council) v National Asylum Support Service*, took Lord Hoffmann as establishing that in interpretation 'an ambiguity need not be established before the surrounding circumstances may be taken into account'.[36] Arden LJ in the Court of Appeal decision in *Static Control Components Ltd v Egan* remarked:

> Lord Hoffmann's principle (1) . . . makes it clear that there are not two possible constructions in any given situation, namely a purely linguistic one and one in the light of the factual background, but only one, the true interpretation. This is because the

35 [1998] 1 All ER 98, pp 114–15.
36 [2002] UKHL 38, [2002] 1 WLR 2956 at [5].

object of interpretation is to discover the meaning of the provision in question in its context . . . Thus, in principle, all contracts must be construed in the light of their factual background, that background being ascertained on an objective basis. Accordingly, the fact that a document appears to have a clear meaning on the face of it does not prevent, or indeed excuse, the Court from looking at the background.[37]

As will be seen, some judges regard contract disputes as resolvable, in theory at least, by the application of 'ordinary grammatical principles' of meaning: literal meaning is the first point of departure.[38] On this view, context only becomes relevant in cases of ambiguity or where the parties have adopted a specialised meaning and so on. The point of contention between the differing approaches relates not to how the interpretative process is to be conducted, but to what interpretation is and when it becomes necessary. Lord Hoffmann subscribes to the 'expansive' view of interpretation – all contracts require contextual interpretation. In Collins' words, Lord Hoffmann is a 'committed contextualist' and, as Collins notes, 'for the committed contextualist, ultimately it is only context that really matters'.[39] For Lord Hoffmann there is no scope for adopting a pure 'meaning of words' approach to the contractual documents. His statement in *Charter Reinsurance Co Ltd v Fagan* confirms this:

I think that in some cases the notion of words having a natural meaning is not a very helpful one. Because the meaning of words is so sensitive to syntax and context, the natural meaning of words in one sentence may be quite unnatural in another. Thus a statement that words have a particular natural meaning may mean no more than that in many contexts they will have that meaning. In other contexts their meaning will be different but no less natural.[40]

Words may still have a literal or conventional meaning, but the courts are not limited to adopting that meaning if the background

37 [2004] EWCA Civ 392, [2004] 2 Lloyd's Rep 429 at [27].
38 See, for example, Staughton LJ in *New Hampshire Insurance v MGN*, *The Times*, 25 July 1995.
39 Collins, 'Committed Contextualism', p 193. See also Smith, S., *Contract Theory*, p 276.
40 [1997] AC 313, p 391.

suggests some other meaning is more appropriate.[41] One advantage of Lord Hoffmann's approach is that courts do not now have to artificially invent ambiguity or vagueness in order to take their enquiries further than the plain meaning of the words. Doubtless Lord Hoffmann was seeking to relieve judges of the necessity of finding ambiguity or difficulty with language before considering the contextual material. Thus in *Sirius v FAI*, the House of Lords did not have to accept what appeared to all of them to be a commercially implausible result based upon natural meaning of the words used – even though there appeared to be no ambiguity in the language. The court could look at the commercial substance of the agreement and circumstances, rather than rely exclusively on the express wording of the contract to determine the result.

It is difficult to deny that all contracts require contextual interpretation to some degree, but, as we have seen, 'context' can be broadly or narrowly defined. The question is whether the shift towards contextual interpretation gives courts greater licence to interfere with the obligations written into the documents in favour of the more elusive understandings generated by the context of the agreement, or the application of policy. The answer is 'not necessarily', but the courts must be alert to the danger of allowing 'contextual interpretation' to be 'interpreted' as giving them greater amending powers. Collins has remarked that Lord Hoffmann's *Investors* speech contains the 'implication that sometimes the text does not matter at all'.[42] Whether contextualism gives judges greater licence to 'construct' agreements really depends upon the remaining role for plain or conventional meaning. In relation to this, it is not the case that literalism and textualism are redundant interpretative strategies that stand in opposition to contextualism; rather, contextualism *subsumes* literalism and textualism. Adopting a strict, plain meaning, or conventional interpretation of a contract may still be appropriate – but only if that is suggested by the wider *social or factual* context of the agreement.

Contextualism subsumes literalism

Lord Hoffmann could be taken to be suggesting that there are no contractual interpretation issues that are dependent for their

41 Lord Hoffmann, *Mannai Investments v Eagle Star Life Assurance* [1997] 3 All ER 352, 380.
42 'Committed Contextualism', at p 199.

resolution upon determining the meaning of words used: whenever a court is determining what a contract means, they can use whatever background information appears relevant. But it would be a mistake to regard contextual and plain meaning approaches as being in opposition, with the result that a judge adopting the contextual approach can thereby *ignore plain meaning*, and engage in reconstruction of the parties' agreement, utilising whatever background information a reasonable person would regard as relevant. Such an approach would certainly have implications for the power balance between the parties and the courts. This overlooks the possibility that the context of the agreement might suggest the parties intended a plain meaning to attach to the documents.[43] A judge that failed to consider this possibility would misunderstand contextual interpretation.

To illustrate the difficulty here, consider the case of *BCCI v Ali*, where Lord Hoffmann delivered an important dissenting judgment.[44] An employee of a bank, Mr Naeem, was made redundant following a reorganisation of the business. In addition to his various redundancy payments he received an extra payment in return for signing a release form. The form stated that:

> The Applicant agrees to accept the terms set out in the documents attached in full and final settlement of all or any claims whether under statute, Common Law or in Equity of whatsoever nature that exists or may exist and, in particular, all or any claims rights or applications of whatsoever nature that the Applicant has or may have or has made or could make in or to the Industrial Tribunal, except the Applicant's rights under the Respondent's pension scheme.

It is well known that the bank later collapsed after the exposure of widespread corruption by some senior managers and employees. In a different case the House of Lords had recognised that, in principle, innocent ex-employees, who faced difficulties in the labour market because of their association with the bank, would have a claim for 'stigma damages'.[45] The issue in *BCCI v Ali* was whether Mr Naeem,

---

43 See Katz, A.W., 'The Economics of Form and Substance in Contract Interpretation' (2004) 104 *Col LR* 496, 520–1. Hereafter 'Form and Substance'.
44 [2001] UKHL 8, [2001] 2 WLR 735.
45 *Malik and Mahmud v Bank of Credit and Commerce International SA (in liquidation)* [1997] 3 All ER 1.

and others, were precluded from pursuing such a claim by signing the release form, the stigma claim being undeveloped at the time of their redundancy.

Looking at the wording of the release, it seems to present no great difficulty in meaning. Mr Naeem had signed away his rights to make any claim 'of whatsoever nature that exists or *may exist*'. While context might limit claims 'of whatsoever nature' to claims arising out of the employment relationship, and not unrelated claims, it appeared *just by looking at the words alone*, that Mr Naeem was prevented from pursing the novel claim. Nevertheless, the House of Lords, by a 4:1 majority, held that the release did not prevent Mr Naeem's claim for stigma damages. Lord Hoffmann's dissent was important for two reasons. First, he placed a limit on principle (2) of his restatement. The reference to 'absolutely anything' was qualified by the addition 'that a reasonable man would regard as relevant'.[46] Second, while he reiterates that all interpretation is contextual, he accepts that 'the primary source for understanding what the parties meant is their language interpreted in accordance with *conventional usage*'.[47] Here, he recognises that plain or conventional meaning still has a role in interpretation. This allows him to conclude that 'BCCI is not contending for a literal meaning. It is contending for a contextual meaning, but submitting that while the context excludes claims outside the employee relationship, it includes unknown claims.'[48] For Lord Hoffman, a consideration of the wider background leads to the conclusion that the parties intended the contract to 'mean what it says' *in context*.[49] To hold otherwise would involve the draftsman in an excess of verbiage in trying to achieve comprehensiveness in the clause. Thus Lord Hoffmann criticises the majority in the case for giving 'too little weight to the actual language and background' of the document, which would make the intended meaning clear.[50] Similarly, in *Union Eagle v Golden Achievement* Lord Hoffman took the view that the parties meant what they said in the contract that 'time was of the essence' in a property sale even with regard to a *de minimis*

46 *BCCI v Ali* at [39].
47 Ibid.
48 Ibid., at [65].
49 Wightman, J., 'Beyond Custom: Contract, Contexts, and the Recognition of Implicit Understandings' in *Implicit Dimensions*, 143 at p 158.
50 *BCCI v Ali* at [37].

lapse of 10 minutes after the contractual completion time. This was only decided after looking at context: a volatile property market where certainty was crucial. In this case Lord Hoffmann said, 'in many forms of transaction it is of great importance that if something happens for which the contract has made express provision, the parties should know with certainty that the terms of the contract will be enforced'.[51] He was therefore unwilling to allow equity to intervene and give relief against forfeiture of deposit. As Collins notes, sometimes 'the context tells the judge not to look at the context'.[52]

Not all judges are sensitive to the realisation that plain meaning (in context) still has an important role. By way of contrast, consider Lord Clyde in *BCCI v Ali*. He said:

> On the face of it, if one were to take a strict or literal approach, the words of the agreement seem to include every claim of any kind, whether then identifiable or not, which Mr Naeem might have in any capacity against the bank at any time, then or in the future. But such a comprehensive disclaimer would in my view be a remarkable thing for him to be giving . . .[53]

One can, of course, make a particular interpretation immediately unpalatable by giving it the pejorative label of 'literal'. But it is surely going too far here to say that disentitling Mr Naeem to sue for stigma damages is being unduly legalistic, or is based upon a 'technical interpretation' or shows too much regard for the 'niceties of language'.[54] Lord Clyde suggests that the literal approach dictates an all or nothing conclusion – literalism requires reading the clause as widely as it can possibly be read. It is then of course much easier to denounce such an interpretation as giving rise to wholly unreasonable results concerning the extent of the release. The mistake here is to assume that once one has adopted a literal approach then literalism must operate unchecked, rendering context completely irrelevant. Lord Clyde suggests that a 'literal' reading would imply that the release seeks to exclude liability for all claims of whatever

---

51 [1997] 2 All ER 215, 218.
52 Collins, 'Committed Contextualism', p 193.
53 At [80].
54 Per Lord Steyn, *Mannai Investments v Eagle Star Life Assurance* [1997] 3 All ER 352, 372.

nature.[55] Since that cannot have been the intention of the parties, the literal meaning is rejected, and the majority of the House of Lords substitutes its own 'reasonable' view based on policy factors concerning the fairness of the exchange and who should bear the risk of a change in the law.[56] For Lord Hoffmann the majority confused the question of what the term meant with the question of whether, in the light of their conduct, BCCI should be able to rely on the term. Of course for Lord Hoffmann, once the relevant context has been identified as the 'employment relationship', and not artificially inflated to include *all possible claims* that Mr Naeem might make against the bank, it was plausible that the term meant what it said. Within that context, nonexistent claims were included within the scope of the release. The wholesale rejection of the 'literal' approach in favour of contextualism may therefore lead the courts into error, albeit an understandable one. Judges must therefore be careful not to allow contextualism to become 'another name for construing the contract until one arrives at the result one wants'.[57]

The intentions of the parties

Prior to Lord Hoffmann's statement, the courts seemed agreed that the point of contract interpretation was to uncover the objective intentions of the parties. In *Pioneer Shipping Ltd v BTP Tioxide Ltd*, for example, Lord Diplock said, 'the object sought to be achieved in construing any contract is to ascertain what the mutual intentions of the parties were as to the legal obligations each assumed by the contractual words in which they sought to express them.'[58] Many contract law instruments and codes also make this claim about the primacy of intention, although reference to the 'common' intention of the parties is preferred. Both the UNIDROIT Principles for International Commercial Contracts and the Principles of European Contract Law assert that a contract should be interpreted according

---

55 The Commercial Court recently resisted an attempt to undermine the operation of an exclusion clause by the same tactic of reading it *too* literally: *Mitsubishi Corp v Eastwind Transport Ltd* [2004] EWHC 2924 at [33].

56 Lord Nicholls was perhaps more open about the policy implications of the case, at [35]. See also Brownsword, R., 'After *Investors*: Interpretation, Expectation and the Implicit Dimension of the "New Contextualism"' in *Implicit Dimensions*, 122.

57 Brownsword, R., *Contract Law: Themes for the Twenty-First Century*, p 162.

58 [1982] AC 724, quoted in Lewison, *The Interpretation of Contracts*, p 19.

to the common intention of the parties.[59] However, in relation to the place of intention in interpretation, a doubt emerges, since Lord Hoffmann does not mention the intentions of the parties in his *Investors* statement. Collins has noted this[60] and contrasts it with the position of other judges who accord primacy to the parties' intentions.[61] Of course it could be that finding the 'intentions of the parties' in a commercial contract is synonymous with discovering the commercial purpose of the agreement, or adopting an interpretation that accords with 'business common sense', since most commercial contracting parties will intend (objectively and subjectively) that their agreement is effective to achieve *some* purpose. Thus Lord Wilberforce in *Reardon Smith Line Ltd v Hansen-Tangen* said, 'when one is speaking of aim, or object, or commercial purpose, one is speaking objectively of what reasonable persons would have in mind in the situation of the parties.'[62]

One reason for the omission may be that Lord Hoffmann was trying to avoid the standard rhetorical statements on interpretation that are easy to make, but offer no real insight into the interpretative process. This would be difficult to reconcile with some of his earlier pronouncements on interpretation though. In the earlier *Mannai* decision he said, 'commercial contracts are construed in light of all the background which could reasonably be expected to have been available to the parties in order to ascertain what would objectively have been understood to be their intention'.[63] Why then, does intention not figure in his *Investors* speech, delivered only one month after the *Mannai* judgment? It could be that he does not refer to the intentions of the parties because he regards the search for them as a largely fictitious exercise. The 'real' point of interpretation is to discover what the contract would mean to a reasonable person. The lack of reference to intention might also be a manifestation of the realisation that such intentions are difficult to discern, and may not actually exist within the documents themselves. Recall that Lord Hoffmann has written, extrajudicially, that the subject matter of the contractual interpretation process is often the utterances of 'imaginary' people.[64]

---

59 At Arts 4.1 and 5.101, respectively.
60 Collins, 'Committed Contextualism', p 198.
61 Op. cit., Staughton, Sir C., p 304.
62 [1976] 3 All ER 570, p 574.
63 *Mannai Investments*, p 380.
64 'Intolerable Wrestle', p 661.

Nevertheless, whether imaginary or not, for some interpretation theorists, this lack of primacy accorded to the intentions of the parties would be quite surprising.[65]

Lord Hoffmann should not be taken to be suggesting that intention is of no relevance. Rather the change is one of emphasis: objectivity – the meaning conveyed to a reasonable person – is more important than the parties' intentions. One reason to omit reference to intention is to avoid any possible confusion between adopting a contextual approach to interpretation and admitting evidence of the subjective intentions of the parties. Can contextualism be regarded as involving the claim that subjective intentions matter? If one concentrates on judicial pronouncements, then the answer is clearly no – as far as intention is relevant, it is objective intention that is the key. But it may be difficult to discern the difference between a subjective approach and a heavily contextualised objective approach.[66] Consider this statement of the court's interpretative task by Lord Steyn in *Sirius International Insurance v FAI*:

> The aim of the inquiry is not to probe the real intentions of the parties but to ascertain the contextual meaning of the relevant contractual language. The inquiry is objective: the question is what a reasonable person, circumstanced as the actual parties were, would have understood the parties to have meant by the use of specific language. The answer to that question is to be gathered from the text under consideration and its relevant contextual scene.[67]

Although referring to the 'reasonable person', this person is situated as the parties were, and must be assumed to know at least some of the things that the parties know. This is in reality an uneasy alliance between objective and subjective approaches. Evidently the personal idiosyncrasies and motives of the parties are not a feature to be taken into account, but beyond that, it is not clear what precisely is included and excluded by the reference to a 'reasonable person, circumstanced as the actual parties were'. Indeed the difficulties of

---

65 Kramer, 'Implication in Fact', p 385; Fish, 'There is No Textualist Position', pp 632–3; Raz, J., 'Intention in Interpretation' in R.P. George (ed.) *The Autonomy of Law*, 1996, Oxford: OUP, p 256.
66 Greenawalt, 'Pluralist', pp 576–7.
67 At [18].

drawing these fine distinctions is one reason why there are calls to abandon the rule excluding evidence of prior negotiations in interpreting contracts. This is discussed further in Chapter 3. Given the possibility of confusion between context and subjective intent, it is perhaps wise of Lord Hoffmann to avoid reference to intention altogether. He notes that, as far as communication is concerned, subjective intent cannot be the vantage point of interpretation, since we have 'no window into [the speaker's] mind'.[68] As well as avoiding confusion with subjectivity, the reference to a 'reasonable person', rather than the parties' intentions, has another advantage.

One tends to regard the objective approach to contracts as being wholly exclusive. Under an objective approach, evidence of the individual subjective intentions of each of the contracting parties, their previous negotiations and so on, will be excluded. Evidence of personal motives is likewise irrelevant. But what is often overlooked is that the objective approach has an inclusive aspect that is unconnected to the intentions of the parties, except in so far as it is attributed to them as 'reasonable contractors' in the same factual situation. In *Investors*, Lord Hoffmann stated that the background must be material that is 'reasonably available' to the parties, but it does not actually have to be known by them. The objective approach can add in to the interpretative process information of which the contracting parties were unaware, but which would be available to their reasonable counterparts. For example, in *Prenn v Simmonds* the interpretative question related to the word 'profits'. Did it refer to the profits of a holding company only, or did it include the profits of the entire group – the holding company and its subsidiaries? Reference only to the word in the document admitted of either interpretation. While one relevant context for making the decision was the purpose of the transaction, Lord Wilberforce also accepted that it reflected 'accepted business practice' and 'accounting practice' that 'profits' referred to the consolidated accounts for the whole group of companies, not the individual accounts for the different enterprises in the group. This material would be relevant to context whether the parties were actually aware it constituted 'accepted business practice' or not, provided the reasonable contractor operating under the same factual situation would be aware of it. Lord Hoffmann then, omits to refer to the parties' intentions not because they are unimportant, but because the objective knowledge of the reasonable contractor is more important. Lord Hoffmann does not wish to be taken to be asserting that there is only *one consideration* in interpretation, whether parties' intentions or anything else. This does raise the issue of what kind of information is reasonably available to the parties in terms of business practice and, in particular, what kind of legal knowledge should be attributed to them. This connects to the important issue of choice of the relevant context within which an agreement should be placed.

What is the background or context?

Although dubbed 'contextual interpretation', Lord Hoffmann does not refer to 'context' explicitly in his restatement. Rather, he refers to 'background knowledge', which includes 'absolutely anything [regarded by the reasonable man as relevant]'. While interpretation is *of* the contractual documents, and may in large part be dictated by the documents, it is not limited *to* the contractual documents. It cannot be denied that all communication, and contracting behaviour, takes place in a context. As Lord Wilberforce remarked in *Reardon Smith Line*, 'No contracts are made in a vacuum: there is always a setting in which they have to be placed'.[69] A court rarely, if ever, confines itself solely to consideration of the contractual documents in resolving contract disputes. At the very least the immediate history of the transaction will be placed before the judge, and the judge may hear evidence from the parties themselves. These parties may have had little or no influence over the wording of the contractual documents. In this respect context is impossible to avoid. But much depends here upon how context is understood. One judge's understanding of context will not necessarily coincide with another judge's understanding.[70] One judge may restrict 'context' to largely legal matters, or the basic facts of the dispute, and another judge may take a more expansive approach. Indeed, while the temptation may be to understand context as all those matters not related to the documents or the law, Lord Hoffmann in *BCCI v Ali* said that background was not confined to the factual background, but could include 'the state

---

69 [1976] 3 All ER 570, p 574.
70 See the comments of the Court of Appeal in *Emcor Drake & Scull Ltd v Sir Robert McAlpine Ltd* [2004] EWCA Civ 1733 at [6], criticising the first instance judge for the range of evidence he considered.

of the law'.[71] Some of the difficulties that arise over choice of context are discussed in the next chapter.

In one sense, Lord Hoffmann is simply articulating the process we all go through when we interpret the communications of others. Lord Hoffmann is suggesting we should abandon technical 'rules' of legal interpretation and interpret contracts the way all of us (as reasonable communicators and users of language – not necessarily legal or contractual language) interpret communicative texts and utterances. The shift in interpretative method is more motivated by a desire to bring contractual interpretation into line with the 'everyday' interpretative method used to understand all instances of communication, whether written or oral. Kramer has pointed out that Lord Hoffmann's remarks are based on modern developments in the philosophy of language and the realisation that all meaning and understanding relies on context to some extent.[72] Contextual interpretation is still directed to the words used, but is undertaken by using information that any user of language would have available to them in working out what the contract means. Hence there is no 'conceptual limit' to what can be taken as background (although the law might limit the available evidence largely for pragmatic reasons).[73] This is reinforced when one considers Lord Hoffmann's remark in *Jumbo King Ltd v Faithful Properties Ltd* that 'the overriding objective in construction is to give effect to what a reasonable person rather than a pedantic lawyer would have understood the parties to mean ... if in spite of linguistic problems the meaning is clear, it is that meaning which must prevail.'[74] Understood in this way, the shift to contextual interpretation is not radical in the slightest – it simply demands that contractual interpretation should be undertaken in the same way as any other 'everyday' interpretative exercise.

This assimilation with everyday communication is brought out in relation to the interpretation of 'linguistic' mistakes in the documents. One of the effects of the change in emphasis in interpretation is that contracting parties now need not rely on an action for rectification to

---

71 At para [39].
72 Kramer, A., 'Common Sense Principles of Contractual Interpretation (and how we've been using them all along)' (2003) 23 *OJLS* 173, 177–82. See, also, McMeel, G., 'Language and the Law Revisited: An Intellectual History of Contractual Interpretation' (2005) 34 *Common Law World Review* 256.
73 Lord Hoffmann, *BCCI v Ali*, at [39].
74 [1999] 4 HKC 707 at 727.

amend mistakes (a court order to amend a contract that contains a defect in recording the agreement, the unrectified contract being contrary to what both parties objectively agreed), the process of contextual interpretation can, in some instances, do it for them.[75] In everyday communication we correct linguistic mistakes all the time and many of these errors will not prevent understanding the meaning of the message that is being conveyed. However, this 'rectifying' aspect of interpretation may run counter to the observance of strict formalities required by many legal documents, and may result in a failure to enforce the contractual scheme that was agreed between the parties. In *Mannai Investments v Eagle Star Life Assurance*,[76] the tenant of rented property wanted to terminate the lease because market rents had fallen in the area. Under the term of the lease agreement between the parties, the tenant could validly terminate provided his notice to terminate expired on the third anniversary of the lease commencement date. The lease began on 13 January 1992. To validly terminate the lease, the tenant would have to give notice that expired on 13 January 1995. The tenant made a mistake and gave notice to terminate the lease expiring on 12 January 1995. The landlord claimed the notice was invalid because it didn't comply with the terms of the lease agreement. The Court of Appeal gave judgment for the landlord, but the House of Lords by a 3:2 majority held the notice to terminate was valid. One party may make a mistake in the contractual language, but provided a reasonable person would understand the message they were attempting to convey, the communication will have its intended effect. Crucially, as a matter of 'everyday interpretation', a reasonable landlord would have understood what the tenant was trying to do. In *Mannai*, attention to the background, context or factual situation of the agreement, utilised through the mechanism of interpretation, turned a formally ineffective document into an effective one. The legal context – including consideration of what would formally constitute a valid notice under the terms of the parties' agreement – was not a paramount consideration for the majority. The case was treated as one concerning *interpretation*, rather than *form*. This issue will be considered further in Chapter 4.

75 McMeel, 'Interpretation and Mistake in Contract Law', pp 54–5. See, also, Lord Millett, *The Starsin*, at [192].
76 [1997] 3 All ER 352.

The shift to contextual interpretation 'in context'

What can motivate the desire to assimilate contractual interpretation with the principles of 'everyday' interpretation? Why allow that the formalism suggested by the agreed legal scheme in *Mannai* can be overridden when the social and factual context communicates the tenant's purposes to the landlord sufficiently well? It was earlier noted that one possibility is that Lord Hoffmann is simply taking on board insights developed in the philosophy of language about the importance of context to interpreting everyday communications. On this view there is no such thing as plain meaning divorced from context. Another possibility is that Lord Hoffmann's restatement (and its precursors) is motivated by the recognition that it is the social context that underpins much contractual behaviour, rather than the formal language of the documents. While courts generally regard contextual material as relevant only to the extent that it provides some answer to the question of what the parties meant by the particular words they used in the documents, there is a much wider significance to the general movement towards contextualism.

Accessing the 'real' agreement

Contextual interpretation offers up the possibility for expanding the range of information available to the judge in resolving the dispute. As we have seen, this expansion would be in accordance with much current contracts scholarship that calls for a greater appreciation on the part of courts of the 'social context' of contracting behaviour. This element of the contextualist critique impinges on contract doctrine (the rules as announced and applied by courts) in different ways, but if Collins is correct when he identifies that 'the perennial issue is whether the written document exhausts the obligations of the parties, or whether the recorded agreement is supplemented and qualified by implicit undertakings',[77] then there is a much wider scope for the operation of context than just assisting the judge in

---

77 Collins, H., 'The Research Agenda of Implicit Dimensions of Contracts' in *Implicit Dimensions* at 3. See, also, Posner, E., 'The Parol Evidence Rule, the Plain Meaning Rule and the Principles of Contractual Interpretation' (1998) 146 *U Pennsylvania L R* 533 at 534.

the interpretation of terms in the documents. For the supporters of contextualism, it is argued that the law should recognise that it is simply one form of support system (among others) for contracts; it is not constitutive of them. As a support system, contract law should focus more on the real agreement that the parties have made, not the reduction of that agreement to the written form favoured by lawyers.[78] This 'real agreement' may be generated by fairly elusive criteria, such as the norms and motivations that arise from trade customs, the previous contracting history between the parties and the market in which the parties operate. This version of contextualism demands more flexibility than the rigid doctrinal structure, and a more individualised approach to the parties' dispute. Collins puts the point well:

> If the courts wish to do justice between the parties rather than referee the quality of the lawyers in devising comprehensive risk allocation, they should not attach such weight to the paperwork but concentrate their energies on an investigation of the context, the market conventions, and the assumptions of the parties in framing the core deal.[79]

The recognition of the whole social dimension to contracts and contracting behaviour is well established in the US literature on contracts, and the contextual approach is enshrined in US contracts law. Articles 1–103(a), 1–303 and 2–202(a) of the Uniform Commercial Code point to the importance of commercial practice, specifically course of performance, course of dealing, or usage of trade, in contractual interpretation. The contextual approach is also supported in the US by empirical studies that demonstrate how businesses make little use of written contracts and contract law in their dealings.[80] There is similar, although less extensive, empirical evidence in the UK of the non-importance of contract law to businesses.[81] This work has led one commentator to remark

---

78 For example, Macaulay, S., 'Real Deal' in *Implicit Dimensions*, at 51.
79 Collins, *Regulating Contracts*, p 165.
80 For example, Macaulay, S., ' "Non-contractual Relations in Business: A Preliminary Study", (1963) 28 *American Sociological Review* 55; L. Bernstein, "Private Commercial Law in the Cotton Industry: Creating Co-operation Through Rules, Norms and Institutions" (2001) 99 *Michigan L R* 1724.'
81 Beale, H. and Dugdale, T., 'Contracts Between Businessmen: Planning and the Use of Contractual Remedies' (1975) 2 *Br J Law and Soc* 45.

on the 'devastating empirical finding of non-use' of contract law in regulating agreements.[82]

There is nothing new in the judicial recognition of the importance of the social dimension to agreement making. In *Reardon Smith Line*, Lord Wilberforce remarked that 'In a commercial contract it is certainly right that the court should know the commercial purpose of the contract and this in turn presupposes knowledge of the genesis of the transaction, the background, the context, the market in which the parties are operating'.[83] The kind of material that is uncovered by an appreciation of 'context' can be general (markets, language) or specific to the parties to the transaction (contracting history). Consideration of such contextual factors can uncover information that suggests a strict application of the contract law rules is inappropriate. Cases like *Williams v Roffey*[84] and *Blackpool and Fylde Aero Club v Blackpool Borough Council*,[85] while not strictly cases on interpretation of contracts, offer good examples of the courts adopting a broadly expectations-based approach to agreement and modification, at the expense of application of doctrine.[86] The articulation of the 'contextual' approach to contract interpretation, at the expense of the legal 'baggage', can thus be seen as a part of a trend of growing judicial appreciation of the social context in which all contracting behaviour takes place.

More pragmatically, the contextual approach may also be motivated by a greater availability of contextual material. Large firms may now have sophisticated methods of maintaining records of communications leading up to the formation of 'the contract' and beyond.[87] Staff members change, and firms may wish to be less reliant on 'institutional memory' in relation to important agreements. Oral negotiations may now be replaced by email and other means of recording transactions, which can be relatively easily stored and accessed. The greater appreciation among judges of the social context of agreements, together with the relative ease of access to contextual material, is undoubtedly one reason for the change in interpretative

---

82 Campbell, D., 'Reflexivity and Welfarism in the Modern Law of Contract' (2000) 20 *OJLS* 477 at 480.

83 [1976] 3 All ER 570, 574.

84 [1991] 1 QB 1.

85 [1990] 3 All ER 25.

86 Adams, J. and Brownsword, R., *Key Issues in Contract*, 1995, London: Butterworths, pp 123–4.

87 Baker, P.V., 'Reconstructing the Rules of Construction' (1998) 114 *LQR* 54, at 60.

emphasis. Of course the remaining difficulty is that given the different frameworks for analysis of contractual obligations, the documents may be drafted by, and addressed to, the pedantic lawyer, rather than the contracting parties. So while it seems plausible that the process of contextual interpretation is an attempt to get more closely in touch with the intentions and expectations of actual contracting parties, and not their lawyers, the method of contextual interpretation *of the documents* is a flawed means of achieving this, since it still attempts to reach the parties' 'non-legal' understandings through the artificial filter of the contractual documents.

Interdisciplinarity in law

The increasing sensitivity to the social contexts of agreements may also in part be motivated by the application of 'interdisciplinarity' within the law. Movements such as law and economics, law and society, and law and literature have brought into question, without necessarily resolving, whether law is or can be autonomous from other bodies of knowledge and understanding about how the world works.[88] While these movements differ over what insights for law can be gained by a study of these other disciplines, 'all concur that the legal world is not to be understood on its own terms, but requires the application of some method or substance provided by other disciplines'.[89] While we must take care not to overemphasise the effect of academic work on practitioners – many of whom can be critical of developments in the law as they affect legal practice[90] – many practitioners will come into contact with such work during their education and many judges, especially in the higher courts, will hardly be immune from intellectual developments in other disciplines which impinge upon the law.

European developments

A further context for a change in approach to interpretative method lies in the increased harmonisation of contract law at the European

---

88 Baron, J., 'Law, Literature and the Problems of Interdisciplinarity' (1999) 108 *Yale LJ* 1059, at 1059.

89 Galanter, M. and Edwards, M.A., 'The Path of the Law Ands' [1997] *Wis LR* 375 at p 376. Quoted ibid., Baron, at p 1060.

90 See, for example, Berg, A., 'Thrashing Through the Undergrowth' (2006) 122 *LQR* 354.

level. In comparison with European systems, English law's preference for objectivity and its supposed formalism may be regarded as a weakness. Thus in the latest edition of *Towards a European Civil Code* there is the statement that, 'Historically, the objective approach with its focus on the literal meaning of the words has been the starting point [of interpretation]. This is related to the fact that in legal systems where development has not yet reached an advanced level there is obviously a strong leaning to formalism and therefore an overemphasis of the role of the literal meaning of contract terms'.[91] Similarly, Berger notes the trend away from formalism in Europe. He writes, 'European legal culture is undergoing a radical change from an overly formalistic tradition to a culture that is significantly less formal, less dogmatic and less positivistic than *national legal cultures* in Europe have been'.[92] The move towards contextualism in interpretation may therefore be seen as a way of bringing English law more into line with its European neighbours.

Ewan McKendrick notes that the process of harmonisation requires more attention 'to be given to the rules and principles applied by the courts when interpreting contractual documents'.[93] Parties may use their own standard terms and conditions when engaging in cross-border trade and some uniformity between English and European approaches to interpretation may reduce the capacity for disputes about what these terms mean.[94] A more flexible, contextual, approach to interpretation, rather than a rule-bound and technical method known and understood only by those schooled in the domestic legal system, is more likely to achieve this assimilation. In addition, European contract law instruments such as the Principles of European Contract Law (PECL) adopt a very expansive approach to the material available in undertaking the interpretative exercise, including reference to prior negotiations and

---

91 Canaris, C-W. and Grigoleit, H.C. 'Interpretation of Contracts' in A. Hartkamp, M. Hesselink *et al* (eds), *Towards a European Civil Code*, 3rd edn, 2004, Nijmegen: Kluwer, pp 445, 450.

92 Berger, K.P., 'European Private Law, Lex Mercatoria and Globalisation', in *Towards a European Civil Code*, 43 at p 55, emphasis added.

93 McKendrick, E., *The Creation of a European Law of Contracts – The Role of Standard Form Contracts and Principles of Interpretation*, 2004, The Hague: Kluwer, p 27.

94 Ibid., McKendrick.

common intentions of the parties.[95] These kinds of instruments will be of increasing influence in the push towards harmonisation and globalisation.

This is not to say that important differences do not remain between interpretative approaches adopted in England and elsewhere. Taking the PECL as exemplary of the European approach, McKendrick has pointed out some significant differences. One of these differences is the lack of reference in Lord Hoffmann's statement to the 'common intention of the parties' in favour of the meaning the words convey to a reasonable contractor. European systems tend to support common and actual intentions of the parties (as far as they correspond) in their interpretative approach, although recourse to the 'reasonable person' may occur if there is no discernible common intent.[96] A related point is that the 'common intention of the parties' approach allows the court some power to adjust contracts, even if contrary to literal meaning. This is a power which English courts have traditionally denied exercising. Finally, the range of admissible materials is much narrower in English law.[97] English courts have still not given up the idea that contract interpretation is largely a matter of textual analysis of the contractual documents. While these are still important differences between English and continental approaches to interpretation, the contextual approach at least demonstrates an important shift in attitude.[98] The contextual approach to interpretation allows for a less rigid approach to the court's interpretative task, even if objectivity and limitations on admissible materials remain. While harmonisation and uniformity in law is an ambitious aim for countries with legal systems grounded in different legal 'families', there can at least be a movement towards uniformity of approach, if not uniformity of expression in the way the rules are formulated. However, the common law approach has its defenders. Lord Falconer, the Lord Chancellor, in his opening speech to a European Contract Law Conference in London on 26 September 2005, after remarking that 'blanket harmonisation

95 For example, Art 1:105, 5:102 Principles of European Contract Law (PECL); see, also, Art 1.9 UNIDROIT Principles of International Commercial Contracts, 2004.
96 Op. cit., Canaris and Grigoleit, p 447.
97 Op. cit., McKendrick, *The Creation of a European Law of Contracts*, pp 31–2.
98 See, for example, the speech of Arden LJ in *ProForce Recruit Ltd v The Rugby Group Ltd* [2006] EWCA Civ 69 at [57].

across the EU of contract law, or any other sphere of law, will not work' stated that:

> the English common law of contract is now a world-wide commodity. It has become so because it is a system that people like. It provides predictability of outcome, legal certainty, and fairness. It is clear and built upon well-founded principles, such as the ability to require exact performance and the absence of any general duty of good faith.[99]

To the extent that contextual interpretation is seen to interfere with these virtues of common law method, its further development must be seen as a controversial matter. Indeed, one of the pressing current issues for the law of contract is whether, and how, it should respond to these realisations concerning social dimensions of agreements, European influence and so on. It is arguable that in the light of disagreement over these issues, the self-regulation of the parties may become more important in relation to interpretative method. This is further explored in Chapter 4.

Conclusion

The significance of Lord Hoffmann's speech lies in its recognition that all understanding relies upon context to a greater or lesser extent, and that contractual interpretation is no different. The 'reasonable person', in deciphering communicative utterances, utilises all necessary background knowledge to access meaning. Thus a plain meaning or literal approach is not an alternative to contextual interpretation, but can only be understood as operating within contextual method. On the whole, the new approach is to be welcomed, not least because it can be seen as a reflection of two factors of undeniable importance to modern contract thinking. One of these is the realisation that contracts are first and foremost social phenomena. The other is the increasing European influence over domestic law. Although the shift to contextual interpretation can be seen as part of these wider developments, the method of contextual interpretation, at least as it is applied in contract law, is not without difficulties. Some of these will be explored in the next chapter.

99 Speech available at http://www.dca.gov.uk/speeches/2005/lc150905.htm (accessed 10 January 2006).

Chapter 3

Contextual interpretation: methods and disputes

Lord Hoffmann's speech in *Investors* is now one of the most often cited judicial pronouncements of all, and his statement has been readily accepted by much of the judiciary.[1] Nevertheless, some have sounded a note of caution. In *Beazer Homes Ltd v Stroude*, Munby LJ, clearly alluding to Lord Hoffmann and Lord Wilberforce, remarked, 'Utterances even of the demi-gods are not to be approached as if they were speaking the language of statute. Our task, rather, is to identify, with their assistance, the underlying principles of the common law'.[2] Although judges might be generally agreed that the law on interpretation must be found in Lord Hoffman's speech, there is still plenty of scope for disagreement about what its detail requires. These disagreements may just be a reflection of the endlessly disputed nature of interpretation. Or they may reflect differences of opinion over the judicial role in the contract dispute or differences about what is 'good for business', or concerning what contextual interpretation requires and allows. In this chapter some of the difficulties with Lord Hoffmann's approach to the interpretation task will be examined. Not all of these difficulties arise directly out of the speech, but they occur because of the seeming contradiction between what the contextual approach demands and the limitations imposed by both legal regulation of agreements and common law method.

---

1 Adams, J. and Brownsword, R., *Understanding Contract Law*, 4th edn, 2004, London: Sweet and Maxwell, p 104.
2 [2005] EWCA Civ 265 at [29].

The relevance of context

Not all judges are convinced that a broader contextual inquiry into meaning is always required to interpret contracts, nor that plain meaning interpretative method has been displaced. Sometimes the belief in natural or ordinary meaning manifests itself in simple statements about what judges take to be the interpretative task. Lord Bingham in *BCCI v Ali* said that:

> In construing this provision, as any other contractual provision, the object of the court is to give effect to what the contracting parties intended. To ascertain the intention of the parties the court reads the terms of the contract as a whole, giving the words used their natural and ordinary meaning in the context of the agreement, the parties' relationship and all the relevant facts surrounding the transaction so far as known to the parties.[3]

Other judges are more strident in their defence of the 'meaning of words' approach, regarding a wider contextual process as necessary only in limited circumstances, when 'ordinary grammatical meaning' yields no answer at all, or an answer that does not conclusively determine the case. Lord Mustill in *Charter Reinsurance v Fagan* said:

> I believe that most expressions do have a natural meaning, in the sense of their primary meaning in ordinary speech. Certainly, there are occasions where direct recourse to such a meaning is inappropriate. Thus, the word may come from a specialist vocabulary and have no significance in ordinary speech. Or it may have one meaning in common speech and another in a specialist vocabulary; and the context may show that the author of the document in which it appears intended it to be understood in the latter sense. Subject to this, however, the inquiry will start, and usually finish, by asking what is the ordinary meaning of the words used.[4]

Of course these judges are not denying the importance of contextual meaning, but they do assert that an extensive trawl through the context may not always be necessary before choosing a plain meaning

---

3   [2001] UKHL 8, [8].
4   [1997] AC 313 at p 384.

approach. Saville LJ in *National Bank of Sharjah v Dellborg* said, 'where the words used have an unambiguous and sensible meaning as a matter of ordinary language, I see serious objections in an approach which would permit the surrounding circumstances to alter that meaning'.[5] He expressed concern that the contextual approach would prevent judges adopting the plain meaning without first ensuring the context supported such an approach: 'This would do nothing but add to the costs and delays of litigation and indeed of arbitration'.[6] In *BCCI v Ali*, Lord Hoffmann said that he was 'not encouraging a trawl through "background" which could not have made a reasonable person think that the parties must have departed from conventional usage.'[7] Nevertheless, given the open-ended nature of contextual interpretation, the concern expressed by some judges appears justified.

The concern manifest by Saville LJ is that the express terms in a contractual document can be overturned by contextual evidence affected through the technique of interpretation. The perceived problem may lie with 'altering contractual obligations', rather than 'altering meaning'. The trawl through background might provide material to impute doubt about the intentions of the parties and, once this doubt is raised, the court is then justified in looking for an alternative meaning, even if the words are capable of a plain meaning. Lord Lloyd alluded to the possible implications of this in his sole dissent in the *Investors* case. Of the interpretation favoured by the majority in the case he remarked:

[S]uch a construction is simply not an available meaning of the words used; and it is, after all, from the words used that one must ascertain what the parties meant. Purposive interpretation of a contract is a useful tool where the purpose can be identified with reasonable certainty. But creative interpretation is another thing altogether. The one must not be allowed to shade into the other. So with great respect to those taking a different view, I do not regard the present case as raising any question of ambiguity, or of choosing between two possible interpretations.[8]

5 Unreported, CA, 9 July 1997.
6 Ibid.
7 [2001] UKHL 8, [39].
8 [1998] 1 All ER 98 at 106.

Although Lord Lloyd adopts a 'meaning of words' approach, his method is no less contextual than Lord Hoffmann's. The difference of opinion related to what was a manifestly absurd or unreasonable result. Lord Lloyd's conclusion was that given the natural meaning did not produce a wholly absurd result, there would have to be very compelling reasons to reject the natural meaning.[9] The question of what is an 'absurd result' is not an easy one to answer and much may depend upon whether a layman or a lawyer's view is taken of the relevant provisions. There are probably not many results that are obviously absurd to both lawyer and layman. This is discussed further in the next section.

Reasonable person or pedantic lawyer?

During the course of his dissenting speech in *Investors*, Lord Lloyd considered the objections to adopting the plain meaning of the provision and found them wanting, remarking, 'I suspect that none of these objections would occur to anyone other than a lawyer.'[10] One advantage of 'plain meaning' is that it is the meaning that is available to anyone familiar with the relevant conventions. But of course, the issue then is what the relevant linguistic conventions are taken to be. In other words, in relation to whose point of view is plainness to be judged? This may be a matter to be decided by 'context', but Lord Hoffmann in *Investors* thought the required point of view was that of the reasonable person with the background knowledge available to the parties. Recall that in *Jumbo King* Lord Hoffmann said that interpretation was concerned with giving effect to a reasonable person's understanding, rather than a pedantic lawyer's. It appears, then, that one of the implications for the modern approach to interpretation is that lawyers' understandings and technical meanings are to be discarded in favour of common sense meanings that appeal to the reasonable person with the parties' knowledge. Yet in the *Investors* decision, when Lord Hoffmann seeks to justify his approach, it is

9 Lord Lloyd did not regard it as absurd that the investors should retain all claims against the building society for an abatement of mortgage monies owing, and not just those 'sounding in rescission', since the investor would not have been fully compensated by ICS and might still face an action from the building society for money owing under the mortgages: See Brownsword, R., 'After *Investors*: Interpretation, Expectation and the Implicit Dimension of the "New Contextualism"' in *Implicit Dimensions*, at 119.

10 [1998] 1 All ER 98 at 105.

almost completely by reference to how lawyers would understand the documents, rather than the lay investor. Although the lay investors had the more user-friendly 'Explanatory Notes' to guide them, the explanatory notes were *not* the contract. The contractual documents governed the legal relationship between the parties, and the construction placed upon them was thus vital to the ordinary investor claimants. However, Lord Hoffmann remarked that the relevant contractual document was 'obviously intended to be read by lawyers'.[11] Contractual interpretation may involve the search for the meaning conveyed to a reasonable person, but Lord Hoffmann recognises that many contractual documents are not 'everyday communications'. They are formal documents addressed to lawyers and should be interpreted accordingly. This causes something of an anomaly in Lord Hoffmann's interpretative approach. While he suggests that formal legal documents, affecting the parties' legal rights and obligations, are addressed to and intended to be understood by lawyers, his overall interpretative approach demands that they should be interpreted according to the meaning to be attached to them by a reasonable person in the situation of the parties, and *not* a pedantic lawyer. Arguably it is Lord Lloyd who adopts such an approach in *Investors*. He preferred the plain meaning that suggested itself to the ordinary investors, rather than the meaning suggested to a reasonable person who had his lawyer 'at his elbow'.[12]

The reasonable contractor fared better against the pedantic lawyer in *The Starsin*.[13] The main issue in the case was as to the identity of the contractual carrier (the contracting party) in a bill of lading contract: was it the shipowner or the charterer of the ship? The contention that the contracting party was the charterer was supported by the face of the bill of lading where the port agents had expressly signed as agents of the charterer. However, on the reverse of the bill the standard terms and conditions contained an 'identity of the carrier' clause which stipulated the shipowner as the carrier. Given the inconsistency in the provisions for identifying the carrier, which took precedence? The Court of Appeal, in an attempt to interpret the document *as a whole*, identified the shipowner. The House of Lords held that greater weight should attach to the terms that the parties had written in themselves, rather than the standard terms and

11 [1998] 1 All ER 98 at 115.
12 Ibid., at 104.
13 [2004] 1 AC 715, [2003] UKHL 12.

conditions appearing on the reverse of the form, and that the charterer was therefore the carrier. This was bolstered by a further argument concerning how shippers, consignees, merchants or bankers,
to whom such bills were addressed, would understand the bills of
lading. Such persons would reasonably expect to find some things
out for themselves 'without a lawyer at [their] elbow',[14] including
who the other contracting party was. Lord Hoffmann reasserted that
interpretation was the search for the 'meaning [the document] would
convey to a reasonable person having all the background knowledge
which is reasonably available to the person or class of persons to
whom the document is addressed. A written contract is addressed
to the parties.'[15] Accordingly, the Court of Appeal had been led
into error by adopting the 'lawyerly' method of seeking to interpret
the document as a whole, including the terms and conditions on
the reverse of the bill. Lord Hoffmann remarked:

> In fact the reasonable reader of a bill of lading does not con-
> strue it as a whole. For some things he goes no further than what
> it says on the front. If the words there are reasonably sufficient
> to communicate the information in question, he does not trouble
> with the back. It is only if the information on the front is insuffi-
> cient, or the questions which concern the reader relate to matters
> which do not ordinarily appear on the front, that he turns to the
> back. And then he calls in his lawyers to construe the document
> as a whole.[16]

Lord Steyn echoed these sentiments in *Society of Lloyds v Robinson*,
when he said courts should favour a 'commercially sensible construction . . . Words ought therefore to be interpreted in the way in which
a reasonable commercial person would construe them. And the reasonable commercial person can safely be assumed to be unimpressed
with technical interpretations and undue emphasis on niceties of
language'.[17] Yet in *Deutsche Genossenschaftsbank v Burnhope*[18] he

---

14 Ibid., per Lord Hoffmann at [75].
15 Ibid., at [73].
16 Ibid., at [82].
17 [1999] 1 WLR 756 (on appeal from *Lord Napier and Ettrick v R. F. Kershaw Ltd*)
    at 763. He repeats here sentiments earlier expressed in *Mannai Investments v Eagle
    Star Life Assurance* [1997] 3 All ER 352, 372.
18 [1995] 1 WLR 1580.

took a different (dissenting) view, asserting that a reference to a 'person' in a contract of insurance should be interpreted as including legal persons (corporations) as well as natural persons. He accepted that while the obvious meaning of 'persons' is natural persons, in the context of a contractual stipulation in a commercial setting, the prima facie meaning of persons includes legal persons. The insurers' contrary argument was denounced as 'a literalist argument devoid of any redeeming commercial sense'. The technical meaning, in these circumstances, was to be preferred. What are we to make of this dispute whether lawyerly meanings should be adopted over layman's meanings? The obvious answer is that attention to 'context' will provide the criteria according to which this can be judged. But this really fails to provide an adequate explanation of the variable factors that would rank the layman's understanding above the lawyer's and vice versa. In truth, the difficulties here relate to the problem of *choice of context* and in particular the choice between the often incompatible social and legal contexts of an agreement. Of course one might say that in so far as the parties engage lawyers to draft their agreements, and choose litigation as the manner of solving their disputes, the relevant context shifts from the social, or commercial, one to the legal one. While this would seem to run counter to the direction of Lord Hoffmann's *Investors* speech, it is clear that it is no easy matter to determine upon the right context for interpreting the agreement.

Choice of context

Judges might be agreed that a problem involves 'interpretation' of the text and that this interpretation must be 'contextual', but there may be subtle (and not so subtle) differences over how this process of interpretation is to be conducted and what the ultimate aim of it is. Thus the intention of the parties, the importance of upholding the agreement, the relative importance of the express words of the agreement, the 'reasonable expectations of the parties' and the meaning the text conveys to a reasonable person may all be considerations. This may be dismissed as just a matter of differences in judicial rhetoric, which do not, in the end, alter the substantive interpretative methods that are adopted. Alternatively, there is no reason why all these considerations shouldn't pull in the same direction towards a unified and uncontroversial interpretation that satisfies all these criteria. But tensions are also likely, particularly between the intentions of the parties and the express terms, and between 'upholding the contract' and the 'commercial context'. Context is no more determinate and unequivocal than language. It has already been noted that contractual contexts can be broadly or narrowly construed, with the result that there are different contexts within which an agreement can be placed. In particular, the social and legal dimensions of the contract present two broad and often incompatible contexts. Courts often have to negotiate a difficult path between the obligations as set out in the written documents and the parties' expectations generated by the social aspects of their agreement.

Total Gas Marketing v Arco British[19] is a good example of these sorts of tensions and the difficulty of resolving them satisfactorily. The case raised the issue of whether one party should be able to rely on the non-fulfilment of a condition in order to terminate a long-term contract within a volatile market (energy). The tension between adhering to the written terms and fulfilling the expectations of the parties in what was envisaged to be a 14-year relationship was evident. The House of Lords unanimously decided to uphold the natural meaning of the term 'condition' and allow the escape from what had become a bad bargain for one of the parties. One might say that it was not so much the natural meaning of 'condition' as the *legal* meaning that was upheld by the House of Lords. This illustrates that the relevant context of an agreement might be taken to be a legal one. Nevertheless, some of their Lordships were clearly uncomfortable with the result. Lord Hope, for one, expressed his frustration that there was no way, *within the scheme of the contractual documents*, to find a meaning that would uphold the agreement. He doubted that the contract really captured the intentions of the parties. Although this was not, in the end, treated as an overriding concern – given the unequivocal wording of the documents there was no compromise position – Lord Hope's judgment displays some sensitivity to those factors that may assist in understanding the wider context of the agreement. It is worth setting out the relevant part of his speech in full:

> I confess however that I have reached this conclusion [Total could terminate the contract] with regret. It seems to me most unlikely that the parties to this agreement intended that it should

19 [1998] 2 Lloyd's Law Rep 209.

be capable of being terminated by reason only of the non-fulfilment of the condition about the allocation agreement . . . This was a commercial contract which, to the knowledge of both parties, was bound to involve the seller [Arco] in a good deal of preliminary expenditure in order to provide the facilities which were needed to deliver the gas which was to be supplied to the buyer [Total]. Their bargain was struck against the background of a market for gas which had proved in the past to be extremely volatile. Substantial changes in the open market price of this commodity would be bound to affect the value of the investment by either party in the transaction. One of the purposes of an agreement of this kind is to eliminate the risk of having to carry the burden of such price changes. It is no secret that the reason why the buyer wishes to terminate the agreement is that the market has now turned in its favour. It can obtain gas elsewhere more cheaply than it would have been required to take gas from the Trent reservoir under the agreement. No doubt it will seek to renegotiate a fresh bargain with the seller for the supply of the Trent gas at a more favourable price. The buyer is not to be criticized if the wording of the agreement permits this course. But the Court should be slow to lend its assistance. Commercial contracts should so far as possible be upheld. That is especially so where the party who seeks to preserve the contract has incurred expenditure after it was entered into with a view to performing it in the future over a period of many years. Almost every commercial enterprise depends upon the investment of capital with the expectation of profit in return. Long term commercial contracts are made in order to protect the value of the investment. It is disappointing to find that in this case it has not been possible to construe the agreement in such a way as to provide the seller with the protection which it was designed to achieve.[20]

His Lordship clearly felt unable to depart from the language of the contract, despite his appreciation of the wider social context that could have provided justification for such a departure. On the other hand, it could be argued that the House of Lords in the case showed admirable restraint. In upholding the terms of the written agreement, the court did not interfere with the contractual scheme agreed

---

20 Ibid., at p 223.

by the parties.[21] The issue that is not considered here is how the court decided that the legal context was the correct one within which to interpret the agreement.

An interesting contrast with *Total* is provided by *Rice v Great Yarmouth Borough Council*. In this case a small horticultural business entered into an agreement with a local authority to provide gardening and maintenance services for Great Yarmouth's parks and open spaces. The contract stated that the authority could terminate the contract 'If the contractor commits a breach of any of its obligations under the Contract'. The first instance judge said that a literal interpretation could not be placed on the provision but that a commercial, commonsense, approach should be taken. He said:

> There has long been a tension in the world of contract between an attachment to literal meaning that makes for certainty with all in black and white and the parties knowing exactly where they are and little room for the relative unpredictability of judicial intervention, and a desire to avoid consequences seen as unfair or seen as offending commercial commonsense . . . In the context of a contract intended to last for four years, involving substantial investment or at least substantial undertaking of financial obligations by one party and involving a myriad of obligations of differing importance and varying frequency, I have no hesitation in holding that the common sense interpretation should be imposed upon the strict words of the contract and that a repudiatory breach or an accumulation of breaches that as a whole can properly be described as repudiatory are a precondition to termination pursuant to [the] clause.[22]

The Court of Appeal upheld the judgment. The answer to what seems like an entirely unjustified inconsistency in approach between *Total* and *Rice* is that in reality, there is no such thing as 'commercial' or 'contextual' interpretation understood as a single kind of technique. On being given authorities on the interpretation of termination provisions, the trial judge in *Rice* remarked that none of them '. . . dealt with commercial circumstances having many parallels to those of a local authority and a contractor who is contractually required for a

---

21 Davenport, 'Thanks to the House of Lords' (1999) 115 *LQR* 11.
22 Per Mellor J, quoted in Court of Appeal judgment [2000] All ER (D) 902, at [18].

period of years to provide a wide variety of services on a repetitive basis.'[23] *Total* was undoubtedly a more complex contract in a volatile market between parties of a high level of commercial sophistication. In addition, the parties were of equal bargaining power, and had legal advice. These factors may have suggested that a more formal approach to the interpretation of the contract was appropriate. Here, context has a role in indicating whether a strict or flexible interpretative approach should be taken to the documents. Although precedents play a minor role in interpretation, judges need a clearer framework of considerations for articulating the relevant differences between cases like *Total* and *Rice*. This would provide reasons for why a strict approach is appropriate in one case, but not the other.[24] The obvious response is that even *contextual* interpretation is only concerned with the contractual documents – the legal framework is the only one that is relevant. But given the gulf that may sometimes exist between the lawyer's understanding of the deal and the parties' understanding, an important contextual inquiry must relate to which context is relevant and whether the parties required a strict or flexible interpretative approach to their agreement. In addition, for a fully contextual approach, the authority and role of the documents must be a prior interpretative issue, as the courts have recognised on numerous occasions. Courts frequently look behind descriptions and labels in the documents, choosing to focus on the realities of the contracting parties' circumstances in fixing obligations.[25] Choice of the correct context within which to interpret a provision is therefore important, but courts rarely openly articulate the considerations that incline them towards one context rather than another.

The limitations on contextual interpretation

Subjective and common intentions of the parties

In relation to the wider 'matrix of fact' that surrounds each individual contract, particularly given the width of Lord Hoffmann's

23 Ibid.
24 See also *Carlton Communications plc and Granada Media plc v The Football League* [2002] EWHC 1650. Noted by Mitchell, C., 'Contract: There's Still Life in the Classical Law' [2003] *CLJ* 26.
25 A notable recent example being *National Westminster Bank plc v Spectrum Plus Ltd* [2005] UKHL 41, [2005] 2 AC 680.

formulation of relevant material, it can be difficult to distinguish admissible context from 'declarations of subjective intent'. The difficulty is particularly acute when evidence of context comes by way of oral testimony from witnesses directly involved in formulating and performing the agreement. In these circumstances, one judge's wider reference to 'context' may look to another judge like an examination of state of mind of the parties. This provides another reason for the preference for documentary evidence.[26] Why is evidence of subjective intent excluded? One reason is that contracts are a joint enterprise, dependent upon clear communication. What each party subjectively intended by entering into the bargain, or by framing the obligation in a particular way, is irrelevant because that meaning is not immediately accessible to the other party: we must rely on 'the reasonable meaning conveyed by a party's words and behavior'.[27] In his *Investors* statement Lord Hoffmann refers to 'background', rather than intention. Although 'background' could include all available information, apart from the words of the contractual text, this is qualified since it is not the information available to the actual parties that is of interest, but the information available to the *reasonable* contractor. This maintains the position that subjective intent is not relevant to the process of interpreting the words.

While it is easy to justify the exclusion of the uncommunicated and unavailable intentions of a single party, it is not clear whether the parties' *shared or common intentions* are likewise excluded. Farnsworth for one regards the exclusion of common intent as a mistake. He writes, 'unhappily many commentators . . . have jumped from the premise that a meeting of the minds is unnecessary to the conclusion that the actual intentions of the parties are irrelevant to the process of interpretation'.[28] For Farnsworth, if a common intent can be discerned then 'it ought to be controlling in matters of interpretation regardless of what either party had reason to believe'.[29] In relation to whether common (shared) intentions are disregarded, English law appears to be in some confusion. Lord

---

26 *Per* Clarke LJ in *Emcor Drake & Scull Ltd v Sir Robert McAlpine Ltd* [2004] EWCA Civ 1733 at [6].

27 Barnett, R.E., 'The Sound of Silence: Default Rules and Contractual Consent' (1992) 78 *Virginia L R* 821, at 875–6.

28 Farnsworth, ' "Meaning" in the Law of Contracts', pp 945–6.

29 Ibid., p 951.

Steyn has written, extrajudicially, that 'the purpose of the process of interpretation is not to find what the parties intended but to determine what the language of the contract would signify to an ordinary speaker of English, who is properly informed as to the objective setting of the contract'.[30] He refers to this as the 'philosophical starting point of English law' and it justifies, among other things, the exclusion of prior negotiations. But this primacy attached to fully objective theory appears to leave no room for common intention either, since 'English contract law eschews [subjective consensus] as an object of interpretation.'[31] For Lord Steyn then, interpretation is based on a fully objective approach – the relevant meaning must be available to the reasonable contractor, irrespective of whether it is shared by the contracting parties. Common intent might be excluded on the grounds that it is likely to generate a protracted and difficult-to-resolve dispute about what each party knew about the other's intentions.

On the other hand, some English judges have made comments supportive of common intent, although it is not clear if they are using 'common' as a synonym for 'objective'. For example, Staughton LJ in *Scottish Power Plc v Britoil (Exploration) Ltd* said that 'it is established law first, that subjective evidence of intention by either party is not admissible. I do not regard that as a quirk of English law, justified only by policy considerations. It is justified because the court is looking for the *common* intention of the parties'.[32] By 'common intention' does the judge mean the common actual intentions of the real parties, or the intentions that might have been shared by their hypothetical reasonable alternatives, which are fixed upon by reference to an objective 'contextual scene'? Similarly, Mr Justice Warren in *Cofacredit SA v Clive Morris & Mora UK Ltd (in liquidation)*, when considering the French law of interpretation remarked that, 'As in English law, the exercise of interpretation has as its objective the ascertainment of the common intention of the parties.'[33] He noted that the French preference was for common intention rather than literal meaning,[34] but he regarded as 'exaggerated' the view that

30 Lord Steyn, 'Written Contracts: To What Extent May Evidence Control Language?' (1988) 41 *CLP* 23 at 28.
31 Ibid., at 30.
32 CA, *The Times* 2 December 1997.
33 [2006] EWHC 353 (ChD) at [37].
34 As with the Principles of European Contract Law, Article 5: 101(1).

French and English approaches to interpretation were opposed.[35] However, he did note that a French interpreter 'must search for the intention of the parties themselves and not the intention of reasonable persons in similar context'.[36]

This is not to say that common intent of the parties is never relevant in English law. Common intent may be relevant where words are naturally ambiguous, and courts have referred to prior negotiations to seek out this intent.[37] Traditionally, courts have not been willing to extend this to cases where the parties might have employed a private language if alternative natural meanings of the words they have used were available. In those circumstances the parties were held to natural meaning. Under Lord Hoffmann's principles, if the parties' common intention behind their contractual words corresponds with conventional or obvious meaning, then there is no problem, since such a meaning is available to the reasonable contractor. If it does not correspond with the conventional meaning (for example the parties have decided between them that 'yes' means 'no', 'cat' means 'dog', etc.,), but the meaning is available to the reasonable person from the admissible background information, then again, under Lord Hoffmann's principles, there would not appear to be a problem. *Mannai* perhaps provides an example of such an instance, although it did not involve a jointly held meaning. In that case the tenant could not have argued that, subjectively, by referring to January 12 he really meant January 13. Rather the reasonable landlord, fully apprised of the relevant context, would have understood the tenant's meaning. This turned subjective intent into a reasonable meaning. The difficulty occurs when the 'key' to the non-conventional, but jointly held, meaning is only available through excluded evidence, such as prior negotiations. Such evidence presently remains inadmissible, and the parties' agreement will be interpreted according to conventional meaning, since the parties' 'real' meaning is not available to the reasonable contractor through the admissible 'context'.

Pragmatically, courts may wish to discourage the use of 'private languages' in the creation of contractual obligations in favour of the

---

35 Ibid.
36 Ibid. See also *Svenska Petroleum Exploration Ab v Government Of The Republic Of Lithuania (No 2)* (QBD) [2005] EWHC 2437; [2006] 1 Lloyd's Rep 181. Here, Gloster J had to consider elements of the Lithuanian contract code, which required a search for common intention over literal meaning.
37 *The Karen Oltmann* [1976] 2 Lloyds Rep 708.

meaning that is available to all reasonable persons with knowledge of the 'objective setting' of the agreement. The exclusion of evidence of what the parties really meant could be a way of encouraging contractors to adopt plain meaning in framing their obligations – not an unreasonable requirement if parties want their contract disputes resolved by the courts. As R. Posner has written:

> whether in interpreting a written contract the court should listen to the testimony of the parties as to what they intended when they negotiated the contract may depend upon whether the purpose of contractual interpretation is to recreate the intentions of the parties or to encourage contracting parties to embody their agreement in a clearly written, comprehensive document.[38]

Alternatively, the preference for objectivity and plain meaning could be related to a public policy argument concerning third parties and others who might be affected by the contract. Savile LJ in *National Bank of Sharjah v Dellborg* pointed out that contracts frequently affect third parties. These third parties would most likely be unaware of the surrounding circumstances and hence it is reasonable for third parties to rely on plain meaning. Once one appreciates the different legal and social frameworks of agreements, one can relate this issue about private meanings to the question of who the documents are for, if they are not primarily for the parties. The documents may be for the public benefit of lawyers for record-keeping purposes. Or they may be primarily intended for the future enforcers, managers, employees or other 'agents' of the project to which the documents relate. Berg points out that one of the reasons why contractual documents exist is to leave a record for agents (employees, lawyers) who may have to deal with the contract after the original contracting parties, or original lawyers, have moved on.[39] In these circumstances the rule against private languages is not entirely nonsensical, and the court's approach to trumping private language with objective meaning is more justifiable. A further reason for the objective approach to interpretation is that courts may prefer such 'common understandings' – where reliable evidence of them exists – to be dealt

38 Posner, R., *Law and Literature*, revised edn, 1998, Cambridge, Mass.: Harvard UP, at 210.
39 Berg, A., 'Thrashing Through the Undergrowth' (2006) 122 *LQR* 354, 358–9.

with by alternative mechanisms such as rectification, estoppel by convention or collateral contracts, rather than by the process of contextual interpretation.[40] The latter is concerned with 'construction' of the contract rather than 'amendment'.[41] Courts may wish to prevent parties routinely seeking to upset the terms of the documents by using common intentions via a process of interpretation. The problem here is that courts are not consistent in their approach to what can and cannot be achieved through a process of contextual interpretation. This is examined further below.

Prior negotiations

One of the more settled rules of contractual interpretation is that prior negotiations between the parties, and previous drafts of the contract, are inadmissible in evidence as to what the terms of the contract mean. Lord Hoffmann preserved this rule in his *Investors* statement, while noting that 'the boundaries of this exception are in some respects unclear'.[42] Lord Hoffmann is keen to assimilate contractual interpretation with everyday interpretation of communications, but artificially ruling out certain kinds of information makes this objective difficult to achieve. In 'everyday' interpretation, no relevant background information is deliberately made unavailable. Most scholars seem to think that, as a matter of interpretative theory, previous negotiations must be relevant to contractual interpretation.[43] On the other hand, as a pragmatic matter, there seems to be no reason why interpretation should not be made subject to some rules, including rules as to what is inadmissible evidence.[44] This point loses force, though, since the rule concerning the exclusion of evidence of prior negotiations is not absolute. Evidence of negotiations

---

40 Lord Hoffmann, 'Intolerable Wrestle', p 667.
41 Ibid.
42 [1998] 1 All ER 98, 114–15.
43 See, for example, Chuah, J., 'The Factual Matrix In The Construction Of Commercial Contracts – The House Of Lords Clarifies' (2001) 12 *ICCLR* 294; Kramer, A., 'Common Sense Principles of Contract Interpretation (and how we've been using them all along)' (2003) 23 *OJLS* 173; McLauchlan, D., 'Common Assumptions And Contract Interpretation' (1997) 113 *LQR* 237; McMeel, G., 'Prior Negotiations And Subsequent Conduct – The Next Step Forward For Contractual Interpretation' (2003) 119 *LQR* 272.
44 Op. cit., Posner, R., p 211; Sunstein, C., *Legal Reasoning and Political Conflict*, 168–71.

is permissible for the purposes of deciding what was agreed in an oral contract, in a case for rectification of the written document,[45] or if one party is trying to establish additional obligations by way of collateral contract. A further exception is when the contract is not incorporated into a final document. If, in the absence of formal documents, a contract has to be constructed 'from scratch' from the parties' behaviour, oral negotiations, dealings and so on, then prior negotiations must be relevant,[46] as must subsequent conduct.[47] In relation to issues of precontractual responsibility and formation, courts may find that they have to engage with negotiations rather than a set of concise and complete documents to discover if an agreement ever came into being.[48] Such a task is not easily distinguishable from the task of interpretation. In addition, if agreement has been reached in the course of negotiations on the meaning to be attached to a particular term, provided the term is ambiguous or has no ordinary meaning, evidence of that negotiated meaning is admissible.[49] While evidence of prior negotiations will be adduced to show an agreed meaning if a term is already ambiguous, it will not be adduced to show that the parties placed an alternative meaning on the term if the term is clear on its face. The absurdity of this distinction is one reason advanced in favour of relaxing the rule against admitting prior negotiations as an aid to interpretation.[50] But, as we have seen above, there are arguments in favour of adhering to plain meaning in this sort of case.

Given that evidence of prior negotiations arguably forms a large part of the 'matrix of fact'[51] from which the contextual approach to interpretation draws substance, there must be some other reasons, apart from relevance, why such evidence is excluded. One of the difficulties is that different reasons are advanced for excluding prior negotiations. There are three well-known and interrelated justifications

45 *Frederick E Rose (London) Ltd v William H Pim & Co Ltd* [1953] 2 QB 450, 461.
46 *The Tychy 2* [2001] EWCA Civ 1198 at [29].
47 *Maggs v Marsh* [2006] EWCA Civ 1058.
48 McMeel, 'Prior Negotiations and Subsequent Conduct', 286–7
49 The classic example is *The Karen Oltmann*. A more recent example is provided by *ProForce Recruit Ltd v The Rugby Group Ltd* [2006] EWCA Civ 69.
50 For example, McLauchlan, D., 'The New Law of Contract Interpretation' (2000) 19 *NZULR* 147, 166–7.
51 Per Lord Hoffmann [1998] 1 All ER 98, 114, following Lord Wilberforce in *Reardon Smith Line v Hansen-Tangen* [1976] 3 All ER 570, 575 and *Prenn v Simmonds*, [1971] 1 WLR 1381.

for the exclusion. The first relates to the subjectivity of the evidence. The injunctions against prior negotiations and declarations of subjective intent often appear together (often in the same sentence, as in Lord Hoffmann's restatement) making it difficult to discern if these are two separate restrictions or only one. McMeel for one has questioned whether 'this distrust of subjective opinions infects the related body of evidence concerning prior negotiations'.[52] The second relates to pragmatic grounds, such as the costs of considering such evidence, and the third relates to its relevance or 'helpfulness'. The argument here is that previous drafts and negotiations can shed little light on what the parties intended in the agreement they eventually reached.[53] This reason in particular can be seen as concerned with recognising and maintaining the differing social and legal frameworks of the contractual arrangements. These reasons are examined in turn below.

Subjectivity

In some versions of the exclusionary rule, the problem is not with prior negotiations per se, but with the 'subjectivity' of the evidence produced. The problem is that reliable evidence of prior negotiations is unavailable. Witnesses will tend to give self-serving statements, rather than accurate testimony of what was jointly, and genuinely, intended. Calls for the relaxation of the prior negotiations often assume that relevant negotiations can be straightforwardly distinguished from declarations of subjective intent. For example, McKendrick writes that 'evidence of pre-contractual negotiations should be admissible in evidence unless that evidence relates to the subjective state of mind of the negotiating parties'.[54] These are not necessarily easy things to distinguish, despite the clear difference between the subjective intent of one party and the joint intention of both parties. Lord Nicholls, writing extrajudicially, has recognised that relaxing the prior negotiations rule may allow evidence of the parties' actual intentions to come before the court. But, he asks,

---

52 McMeel, 'Prior Negotiations and Subsequent Conduct', p 274.
53 Per Lord Wilberforce *Prenn v Simmonds*, p 1384; Staughton, Sir C., 'How Do The Courts Interpret Commercial Contracts?' (1999) 58 *CLJ* 303, 306.
54 McKendrick, E., 'The Interpretation of Contracts: Lord Hoffmann's Restatement' in S. Worthington (ed.), *Commercial Law and Commercial Practice*, 2003, Oxford: OUP, 139 at 156. Hereafter, 'Lord Hoffmann's Restatement'.

'Why should it be thought this evidence of the parties' actual intentions, because that is what this is, can never assist in determining
the objective purpose of a contractual provision or the objective
meaning of the words the parties have used?'[55] Prior negotiations
therefore should be admissible if they help shed light on the language
used by the parties. It also seems that documentary evidence, rather
than oral testimony is to be preferred. The latter is to be treated with
some care.[56] It has been noted that these considerations about subjectivity and reliability tend towards the weight to be attached to
the evidence, rather than its admissibility.[57] The parties' own understandings and intentions will form a large part of the factual matrix
or context, and would constitute the 'background' information most
readily accessible and meaningful to the parties. These arguments
seem to make it clear that the theoretical grounds for excluding such
evidence – the grounds that such evidence offends against objectivity
– are not strong when the evidence might be highly relevant to the
interpretation to be placed on the contract.

Costs

The most likely pragmatic ground for excluding evidence of prior
negotiations relates to the costs of considering such evidence when
weighed against its relevance. After all, if the approach to contract
interpretation is now 'contextual' there will be costs involved in
sifting through evidence to decide what is admissible and what is not.
Contextual interpretation has been criticised on the basis that, since
views will differ on what context or matrix includes, it will lead to
increases in the costs of litigation.[58] Pleas to constrain background
material on grounds of cost have been made in *Sharjah v Dellborg*
and *Scottish Power v Britoil*. Judicial expressions of concern over the
range of material coming forward in the guise of 'context' or 'matrix
of fact' are not new, but predate the *Investors* judgment.[59] Judges can
hardly be surprised by this expansion of 'matrix' since 'one of the

---

55 'My Kingdom for a Horse: The Meaning of Words' (2005) 1 *LQR* 577, 581.
56 Ibid., 585.
57 McLauchlan, D., 'Common Assumptions And Contract Interpretation', p 242,
and McMeel, 'Prior Negotiations and Subsequent Conduct', 298.
58 Op. cit., Staughton, Sir C., 307.
59 For example, Staughton LJ in *New Hampshire Insurance Co v Mirror Group
Newspapers Ltd* [1996] CLC 692.

things advocates and barristers are paid for is knowing what is worth trying on and what is not'.[60]

In addition to this, there may also be 'institutional costs', related to the protection of contract doctrines. Much background material may not be relevant to the issue of what the words of the contract mean, but to the question of what obligations were undertaken. There may be a discrepancy between what the words of the contract say and what the parties thought they had agreed. Courts may wish to exclude this evidence as a way of preventing the parties seeking to change the agreed statement of terms through a process of 'contextual interpretation', rather than the more specific doctrines of rectification, collateral contracts or estoppel by convention (which have their own requirements and limitations). It was noted in Chapter 1 that the process of interpretation might be difficult to distinguish from other processes. Courts differ in how rigidly they maintain the distinctions between different doctrinal techniques of contract law. For example Goff J in *Amalgamated Investment & Property Co Ltd v Texas Commerce International Bank Ltd*,[61] drew a clear distinction between interpretation of contracts and estoppel. The defendant bank sought to enforce a guarantee it claimed had been made in its favour. The wording of the guarantee made it plain that it was a subsidiary of the bank that was to receive any money payable under the guarantee. Goff J held that, as a matter of interpretation, the plaintiffs were not liable to the bank, but only the subsidiary. This was notwithstanding that the contextual evidence demonstrated that all the parties understood the guarantee was in favour of the bank. Goff J was prepared to hold that the plaintiffs were estopped by convention from denying liability to the bank. The Court of Appeal, on the other hand, was prepared to concede, as a matter of interpretation, that the guarantee was in favour of the bank. For Lord Denning there was not much difference between applying the doctrine of estoppel by convention and interpreting the contract in relation to the course of dealing undertaken by the parties. He remarked:

> If parties to a contract, by their course of dealing, put a particular interpretation on the terms of it – on the faith of which each of them – to the knowledge of the other – acts and conducts

---

60 MacCormick, *Legal Reasoning and Legal Theory*, 199.
61 [1982] QB 84.

their mutual affairs – they are bound by that interpretation just as much as if they had written it down as being a variation of the contract.[62]

Similarly, cases of mistaken identity[63] and errors in the documents[64] have been treated as matters of contractual construction. Access to prior negotiations may be disallowed to prevent the parties routinely seeking to undermine the integrity of the documents through a process of contextual interpretation.

Helpfulness, relevance and the legal framework

Lord Wilberforce in *Prenn v Simmonds* maintained that the main reason for the exclusion was:

> simply that such evidence is unhelpful. By the nature of things, where negotiations are difficult, the parties' positions, with each passing letter, are changing and until the final agreement, though converging, still divergent. It is only the final document which records a consensus.[65]

In this passage there lies a recognition of the different frameworks operating within a contractual relationship. In relation to the exclusion of prior negotiations, it is arguable that the law excludes such information to avoid the problem of narrative dislocation. Such information that might be gleaned from negotiations would be more at home in the narrative of the social relationship rather than the context with which the law is concerned – the explication of legal rights and duties, and their enforcement in terms of orders to pay damages and so on. The exclusion of prior negotiations as 'irrelevant' simply reflects the autonomy of law from this social framework. In excluding prior negotiations, courts are recognising (or imposing) a view that such material represents a different 'context' with which they are largely not concerned. Judge LJ in *National Bank of Sharjah v Dellborg* put the point well:

---

62 Ibid., p. 121.
63 *Shogun Finance Ltd v Hudson* [2003] UKHL 62, [2003] 3 WLR 1371.
64 *Mannai Investment Co Ltd v Eagle Star Life Assurance Co Ltd* [1997] 3 All ER 352.
65 [1971] 1 WLR 1381, p 1384.

The negotiations which culminated in the written agreement no doubt reflected the complication and difficulty of the litigation itself. Each party would have conceded some points in order to encourage or benefit from concessions by the other party. Some concessions may have been withdrawn after they had been made and no doubt the position maintained by each party varied, sometimes becoming more flexible and sometimes less. If the realities involved in settling litigation are borne in mind attention to the course of negotiations and material disclosed or exchanged for that purpose will self-evidently, to use the word applied by Lord Wilberforce in *Prenn v Simmonds* [1971] 1 WLR 1381, be 'unhelpful'.[66]

Savile LJ in *Sharjah* also pointed out that one should not confuse 'what is agreed with the circumstances in which it was agreed'. He was prepared to concede as a 'theoretical proposition' that there was a difference between prior-contractual evidence, which demonstrated a fact of common knowledge, and evidence of the parties' negotiating position, which was likely to change as negotiations proceeded. But he also noted that there was an important difference to be maintained between what a person knows and what he intends to undertake as a matter of contractual or legal obligation. Staughton LJ in *Scottish Power v Britoil* said that 'negotiations represent what one party or the other hopes to achieve, not what the contract "actually" means'. A judge's view of the negotiating process may be that each side is trying to gain the balance of advantage in the final deal: the parties are adversaries, not engaged on some common co-operative enterprise.[67] In taking this view, the courts are also mindful of the stage at which they are hearing such evidence. The judge is notionally searching for what the parties meant by their words when the contract was made.[68] The view of contract as a co-operative endeavour can easily be obscured from the judge embroiled in litigation, particularly when the parties precisely disagree about what the contract means. Since the law views the parties as adversaries both at the stage of negotiation and litigation, it

---

66 Unreported, CA, 9 July 1997.
67 The classic statement along these lines being from Lord Ackner in *Walford v Miles* [1992] 2 AC 128.
68 Per Lord Parmoor, *Union Insurance Society of Canton Ltd v George Wills & Co* [1916] 1 AC 281, cited in Lewison, *The Interpretation of Contracts*, 89.

tends to rely only on the objective evidence of the documents as representing a consensus.

Subsequent conduct

Generally, evidence of how the parties conducted themselves after the contract was made and during performance is not admissible in deciding how contract terms should be interpreted. If the parties' conduct after their agreement makes it clear they both placed a particular interpretation on their contract *from its inception*, why should a court ignore this highly relevant evidence? Lord Nicholls has recently questioned the rule, both in judgments and extrajudicial writing,[69] but the rule has also been defended by Arden LJ in the Court of Appeal. She noted that the law did not presently allow consideration of subsequent conduct, and that the rule was justified on the grounds of certainty:

> When it comes to legal policy it is important that the law should not undermine the certainty of the meaning of contracts or lead to a position where the meaning of a contractual provision fluctuates according to the conduct which in fact occurs under the contract when it is performed by the time the meaning has to be ascertained. It is therefore worth repeating and emphasising that the courts in general should not have regard to subsequent conduct when interpreting written contracts.[70]

As with all these rules there are exceptions, such as the doctrine of waiver, post-contractual variation and estoppel by convention.[71] Subsequent conduct may be evidence of a course of dealing, which could give rise to additional, independent obligations from the original contract.[72] In addition, while subsequent conduct is inadmissible for the purposes of interpreting a written contract, it is relevant for the purposes of deciding what obligations the contracting parties

69 In *BCCI v Ali*, and 'My Kingdom for a Horse', respectively.
70 *Full Metal Jacket Ltd v Gowlain Building Group Ltd*, [2005] EWCA Civ 1809, at [17].
71 *Amalgamated Investment & Property Co Ltd v Texas Commerce International Bank Ltd*. Lord Denning was clearly of the opinion that there ought to be no bar to use of subsequent conduct in matters of interpretation, although he was prepared to accept the existence of the rule disallowing it: [1982] QB 84, 119.
72 Ibid., per Lord Denning.

undertook in an oral or partly oral contract. However, there appears to be some confusion about the role of evidence of subsequent conduct here. The Court of Appeal has recently asserted that such evidence is examined not for the purposes of ascertaining the original obligations – the court's task is still to ascertain what the parties agreed at the time they made the oral contract. Evidence of what the parties subsequently did or said in relation to the matters that they now dispute may be relevant in assessing which party's recollection of the events at the time of the agreement is to be preferred.[73] The courts still hold the view that there is a fixed point in time at which the extent of obligations, and their meaning, is assessed. Subsequent conduct assists in testing the veracity of witnesses on this issue, not for the purpose of deciding terms.[74]

Relaxation of the exclusionary rules

The prior negotiations rule was reasserted by Lord Hoffmann in the Privy Council decision of *Canterbury Golf International Ltd v Yoshimoto*.[75] In that case, the New Zealand Court of Appeal had relaxed the prior negotiations rule to admit previous drafts of a contract for the purposes of interpretation. Lord Hoffmann maintained that the evidence in that case should have been excluded because it was unhelpful, rather than for considerations of practical policy.[76] This suggests that, in the future, helpful evidence might be included, although it is unclear what the criteria of helpfulness are. Commentators, and some judges, have noted that the continued general exclusion of prior negotiations is difficult to reconcile with the contextual approach to interpretation that Lord Hoffmann advocated in *Investors*. Arden LJ in *ProForce Recruit Ltd v The Rugby Group Ltd* remarked that the exclusion was:

> not on the face of it consistent with the general principle that a contract should be interpreted in the light of its context. Nor, on the face of it, is the application of a meaning which is not that

---

73 See op. cit., recent Court of Appeal decision in *Maggs v Marsh*, esp [24]–[26].
74 *Contra*, see Lewison, *The Interpretation of Contracts*, pp 89 and 91, who supports the view that subsequent conduct may be relevant for deciding what the terms were.
75 [2002] UKPC 40.
76 Ibid., [25].

which the parties themselves gave to a term consistent with the general approach of contract law, which is to respect party autonomy.[77]

McKendrick has pointed out the difficulties of drawing a distinction between prior negotiations and 'context' and he concludes that 'in principle, evidence of pre-contractual negotiations should be admitted, even if, in many cases, it ultimately proves to be "unhelpful" '.[78] Kramer also recommends that, if not justified on policy grounds, the rule should be abolished because it is 'inconsistent with the common sense principles of everyday interpretation' and so 'prevents contracts being given the meaning that they were intended to take'.[79] On the other hand, while such exclusions seem antithetical to a fully contextual approach to contracts interpretation, some would argue there is no reason why interpretation cannot proceed on the basis of 'rules'. Richard Posner argues that a general theory of interpretation is neither possible nor desirable since interpretations are always sensitive to the purposes of the enterprise. So if contract law adopts a relatively 'narrow textualism' in interpreting contractual documents, this is because '[t]he principles of contractual interpretation depend on the purposes of contract law, rather than on any general theory – there is no such thing – of interpretation'.[80] On this basis, while placing limits on the admissible information (or employing a 'stopping rule'[81]) may be difficult to justify on principled grounds, it may be fully justified on pragmatic grounds that are unrelated to what it means to 'interpret'. On this issue, Fish points out that, 'stopping rules are not rules of interpretation, but rules that tell you when the effort to interpret should cease and something else should take over'.[82]

Recent reactions from the Court of Appeal on the future of the prior negotiations rule have been mixed. The Court of Appeal recently reasserted the rule in fairly robust terms in *Beazer Homes Ltd v Stroude*. This case in particular throws up the pragmatic difficulties

---

77 [2006] EWCA Civ 69 at [57].
78 McKendrick, 'Lord Hoffmann's Restatement', 157.
79 Op. cit., 'Common Sense Principles of Contract Interpretation', 180.
80 R. Posner, *Law and Literature*, 246.
81 Vermeule, A., 'Three Strategies of Interpretation' (2005) 42 *San Diego L R* 607, 612.
82 Fish, 'There is No Textualist Position', p 640.

presented when a seemingly clear rule about the admissibility of evidence is thrown into doubt. In *Beazer* the first instance judge held a preliminary hearing on admissibility before hearing an application for summary judgment. One of the Court of Appeal judges remarked:

> In general, disputes about the admissibility of evidence in civil proceedings are best left to be resolved by the judge at the substantive hearing of the application or at the trial of the action, rather than at a separate preliminary hearing. The judge at a preliminary hearing on admissibility will usually be less well informed about the case. Preliminary hearings can also cause unnecessary costs and delays.[83]

The court thought there was no advantage for anyone in having the preliminary hearing as to admissibility. Counsel was evidently pushing the boundaries of the rule since the evidence of negotiations he sought to admit related to a different contract than the one in dispute. The case for admitting such evidence was very weak indeed. Mummery LJ said:

> Like much material that is irrelevant or only marginally relevant, this evidence is distracting and detrimental to the legal process: it is time wasting, cost consuming and diverts attention away from what matters most when construing a formal written contract, namely, the language which the parties have agreed upon to express their contractual intentions.[84]

He denounced the evidence as 'quite simply worthless'.[85]

The Court of Appeal in the case of *ProForce Recruit Ltd v Rugby Group* demonstrated a more liberal approach.[86] This was an appeal against a striking out order, so the case did not provide an opportunity for consideration of all the substantive issues. The court only considered if the claimant had a real prospect of success at trial. Nevertheless, despite its limited precedential value, the case is worthy of attention. ProForce was an employment agency that had supplied temporary workers to Rugby since 1997. In July 2001, the parties

83 Per Mummery LJ [2005] EWCA (Civ) 265, at [10].
84 Ibid., at [26].
85 Ibid.
86 [2006] EWCA Civ 69, at [19]–[20].

entered into a written service agreement for ProForce to supply cleaning staff to Rugby. One term stated that: 'This contract will be of a minimum two-year period and will be re-negotiable at the end of that period. During that period ProForce will hold preferred supplier status.' In November 2001, Rugby began using other employment agencies to meet its staffing needs. ProForce claimed that 'preferred supplier status' meant that they had the legally enforceable right of first refusal in supplying workers and equipment of any kind to Rugby, not just cleaning staff, and that Rugby had breached the contract. To support their interpretation, ProForce sought to adduce evidence from their chairman and managing director. This was to the effect that, during negotiations with representatives of Rugby, all the parties understood that 'preferred supplier status' meant that ProForce was to supply workers to Rugby in preference to other suppliers, and that no other supplier would be approached until ProForce had been given a reasonable opportunity to meet Rugby's needs. ProForce also claimed that the change in Rugby's policy had been prompted by a change from the staff at Rugby who had negotiated the agreement. The case is therefore a good example of the 'agency' problem referred to earlier.[87] The position was complicated by the presence of an 'entire agreement clause' in the contract, which seemingly precluded reference to negotiations in determining the parties' obligations.

The trial judge had ruled the evidence of negotiations inadmissible, and that 'preferred supplier status' meant simply that if Rugby chose to operate a system of preferred suppliers, ProForce would be one of these for all categories of workers, not just cleaners. However, the term did not oblige Rugby to operate a 'preferred supplier' system, nor to contract only with ProForce. ProForce argued that this interpretation would render the term meaningless – its inclusion in the contract must have meant *some* legal obligation attached to it. The Court of Appeal disagreed with the trial judge and said that the interpretation issue should proceed to trial. Mummery LJ noted that the words did not have a plain or ordinary meaning, and nothing about its meaning could be extracted from the rest of the document, nor were there any useful precedents. Since the term lacked an obvious interpretation, this was a case where the negotiations might well shed light on the parties' intended meaning. He remarked:

---

87 See text accompanying note 38.

It would be necessary to explore the factual hinterland of the agreement in order to see whether illumination of the meaning of the expression could be found: for example, in evidence showing that the parties had agreed upon the meaning of the terms or had a mutual understanding of the term and were using it in the agreement as a shorthand expression of their agreement or understanding.[88]

Arden LJ agreed that this might be a case where prior negotiations were relevant. She said:

These words are undefined and they are not introduced or accompanied by any words of explanation. In those circumstances it is in my judgment reasonably arguable that on their true interpretation those words bear the meaning that the parties in common gave them in their communications leading up to the signing of the agreement.[89]

This would seem to be an acceptance of the relevance of common intent, supported by evidence of what took place during negotiations. Arden LJ also drew support from Lord Nicholls' extrajudicial opinions on the issue.[90]

On the face of it, *ProForce* looks like a case where prior negotiations would be helpful. But the case also illustrates some of the difficulties with relaxing the exclusionary rule. There was only a single witness able to give evidence of what had transpired during the negotiations, the chairman and managing director of ProForce, and he was, of course, likely to give evidence that supported his case. Others who negotiated the contract on behalf of Rugby had left the company by the time of the litigation. Of course, given the nature of the proceedings in this case, the court had to assume that ProForce could prove their allegations at trial, and it must be recognised that ProForce face a heavy evidential burden. In addition, such contextual material (negotiations) is itself open to interpretation and may present its own interpretative difficulties. Oral evidence may be self-serving; documentary evidence of negotiations may be no more reliable than the written contract that arose from them. Of

88 [2006] EWCA Civ 69, at [28].
89 Ibid., at [55].
90 Op. cit., Lord Nicholls, 'My Kingdom for a Horse'.

course the argument in response is that these considerations go to the weight of the evidence, not its admissibility. But it may prove difficult for judges to dismiss such evidence from their minds once they have heard it, even if it is judged not to be of sufficient weight to affect the outcome. Arden LJ thought an express term that said that prior negotiations were admissible would be upheld, yet it is arguable that the parties had attempted to oust prior negotiations from consideration by use of an entire agreement clause. If the rule is relaxed, and all the indications are that it has been, it must be open to the parties to take their own steps to exclude such evidence from the court's consideration. This possibility is discussed further in Chapter 5.

Wider developments

A cursory glance at some international instruments and contract codes reveals some very expansive approaches to interpretation being advanced, including reference to prior negotiations and subsequent conduct.[91] The Principles of European Contract Law, the UNIDROIT Principles of International Commercial Contracts 2004 and the United Nations Convention on Contracts for the International Sale of Goods 1980 (the Vienna Convention) all allow reference to a wider set of materials in interpretation than have traditionally been used by the English courts. While the first two of these are optional terms the parties are free to incorporate into their agreement, and the Vienna Convention has not been ratified by the UK, these instruments demonstrate the possible future direction of the law on interpretation. In her judgment in *ProForce*, Arden LJ said that account should be taken of these instruments and she hinted that the objective approach of the common law might need reconsideration.[92] The UNIDROIT principles state in Art 4.1 (1) that 'A contract shall be interpreted according to the common intention of the parties.' It is only if such a common intention is not discernible that the perspective of the 'reasonable person' in the position of the parties is used. In Art 4.2, statements and conduct of a party are 'interpreted according to that party's intention if the other party knew or could not have been unaware of that

---

91 For example, PECL Art 5.102; McKendrick, 'Lord Hoffmann's Restatement', 162.
92 [2006] EWCA Civ 69, [57].

intention'. Art 4.3 allows regard to be had to all the circumstances in interpretation including:

(a) preliminary negotiations between the parties;
(b) practices that the parties have established between themselves;
(c) the conduct of the parties subsequent to the conclusion of the contract;
(d) the nature and purpose of the contract;
(e) the meaning commonly given to terms and expressions in the trade concerned;
(f) usages.

The Principles of European Contract Law follow a similar line. Article 5:101 states that a 'contract is to be interpreted according to the common intention of the parties even if this differs from the literal meaning of the words'. A similar expansive approach to the material relevant to interpretation is also taken, with additional reference to good faith and fair dealing.[93] Although these measures might be thought presently to fall into a benign category, with the European Commission's *Communication on European Contract Law*,[94] the subsequent *Action Plan*[95] and *The Way Forward*[96] document, it is clear that the harmonisation project has become more ambitious, even if the proposals still fall short of advancing a 'one size fits all' body of contract law rules applicable across Europe. Nevertheless, a degree of uniformity in contractual interpretation may be necessary to the harmonisation project, and some relaxation in relation to the admissible materials would be a significant step in this direction.

Conclusion

Contextual contractual interpretation presents dilemmas concerning the choice of relevant context within which to place an agreement,

93 Art 5:102. See also Article 8(3) of the Vienna Convention.
94 *Communication From The Commission To The Council And The European Parliament On European Contract Law* COM (2001) 398, [2001] OJ C255/01.
95 *Communication From The Commission To The European Parliament And The Council, A More Coherent European Contract Law: An Action Plan* COM (2003) 68, [2003] OJ C63/01.
96 *European Contract Law and the Revision of the Acquis: The Way Forward* COM, 2004, 651.

whether 'plain meaning' approaches are still possible, whether and how intentions are relevant, and what evidence is admissible in the interpretation exercise. Of course, the inherently flexible quality of 'context' can be presented as its main advantage. Attention to context allows the courts greater sensitivity to individual contracting circumstances and the ability to tailor interpretations to the actual contractual situation of the parties. The weakness of contextualism is its unpredictability. Parties, and their lawyers, may appreciate that their contract will be interpreted 'contextually', but have little idea of what outcomes this may lead to, since they may be unaware of what particular context, and contextual material, is regarded as controlling by the court. Given this uncertainty, the possibility presents itself that some parties may prefer a more formal interpretative method to be applied to their agreement. This is considered in the next chapter.

Chapter 4

Formalism in interpretation

In this chapter, the position often taken to be opposed to contextualism in contract interpretation – formalism – is considered. If contextualism requires looking outside the text of the legal documents in interpretation – perhaps even outside the law and legal framework – then formalism describes the tendency 'to decide cases on narrow grounds of the inner logic of the law'[1] or to adopt 'overly rule-bound decision making'.[2] Literalism in contract interpretation is often associated with formalism, since literalism regards the words of the text as the best means to access the parties' intentions, and to give the words their plain meaning as the best way of effectuating those intentions.

Any extended discussion of formalism poses an immediate problem. Formalism is notoriously difficult to define, being very often a thinly veiled term of abuse for any number of controversial views about legal reasoning.[3] It is difficult to come up with any clear exposition of formalist doctrine in contract law.[4] Formalism in contract might be manifest by the mechanical application of the rules and doctrines of classical contract law, such as strict adherence to the requirement of consideration or a strict application of the parol evidence rule or the third-party rule, however unjust the results might be. In relation to the language of contract documents, formalism might be 'the thesis that it is possible to put down marks so

---

1 Lord Steyn, 'Does Formalism Hold Sway in England?', 44.
2 Stone, M., 'Formalism' in J. Coleman and S. Shapiro (eds), *The Oxford Handbook of Jurisprudence and Philosophy of Law*, 2002, Oxford: OUP, 166, 173.
3 Schauer, F., 'Formalism' (1988) 97 *Yale LJ* 509, 510.
4 However, see the explanation in Adams and Brownsword, *Understanding Contract Law*, 4th edn, pp 185–7.

self-sufficiently perspicuous that they repel interpretation'.[5] On this view, formalism is not a method of interpretation; it is the antithesis of interpretation. It has already been argued that the shift to contextual interpretation may in part be motivated by the greater appreciation of the social aspects of contracting behaviour. Formalism, on the other hand, seems precisely to require 'the separation of law from life, of the meaning of the text from its context'.[6] But it has also been noted that all interpretation is context-dependent to some degree. Any formalist interpretation that seeks to deny any role for context can be very easily dismissed. Although much depends upon what is meant by context, it is difficult to detect anyone holding to the position that contract interpretation can proceed with reference to *nothing but* the documents – given the indeterminacy of language every contractual text has the capacity for ambiguity. It is rare, and arguably impossible, for a judge to give a completely acontextual interpretation of the words of a contract. As Sunstein remarks, 'formalism is a doomed enterprise if it is an effort to give meaning to terms apart from cultural understandings and context'.[7] On this basis, clear words are only clear because everyone understands the context in which they are operating. Rather, the hallmark of a more serious kind of formalism in contract would be the tendency to regard the contractual text as supreme evidence of the parties' intentions, over more elusive and equivocal evidential material, such as trade customs, previous dealings and so on, and adhering to plain meaning, except when the context unequivocally suggests some different outcome was intended. Of course judges may still disagree over what constitutes an 'unreasonable' or 'commercially ridiculous' result, but one of the issues here is whether judges should be the arbiters of what is unreasonable or absurd. Judges frequently disagree over this question, occasionally pointing out that there is no law that says contracts have to be reasonable.[8] Given these difficulties, the argument is that the decision as to interpretative strategy is

---

5   Fish, S., *There's No Such Thing as Free Speech: And it's a Good Thing Too*, 1994, New York: OUP, 142.

6   Ben-Shahar, O., 'The Tentative Case Against Flexibility in Commercial Law' (1999) 66 *Univ Chi L R* 781, 781.

7   Sunstein, C., 'Must Formalism be Defended Empirically?' (1999) 66 *Univ Chi L R* 636, 645.

8   For example, Staughton LJ in the Court of Appeal decision in *Charter Reinsurance v Fagan* [1996] 1 All ER 406; Lord Reid in *L Schuler AG v Wickman Machine Tool Sales Ltd* [1973] 2 All ER 39 at 45.

best left to the parties. In this chapter the concern is not with a formal or literal approach to contractual obligations understood as opposed to a contextual approach, but as an interpretation method the parties might choose. The different justificatory arguments for formalism are examined and some of the broad reasons why parties may prefer more formal interpretation methods are considered.

Formalism in contract

It is tempting, but mistaken, to brand as 'formalist' anyone disagreeing with the general idea of contextualism. One need only consider the dissenting judgments in cases such as *Investors, Mannai* and *BCCI v Ali* to see that such polarisation of views is nonexistent. Indeed, most judges would agree that contractual interpretation involves extracting the objective meaning of *a text*. This understanding would mark English contractual interpretation as relatively formalist compared with some other jurisdictions. Even Lord Hoffmann's restatement is formalist in the sense that he regards contextual interpretation as a technique to be applied *to the contractual text*. In addition, by excluding some potentially relevant evidence (prior negotiations) from his elucidation of context, even if this exclusion was not unequivocal, he accepts the operation of an established rule that artificially restricts the available contextual material. For some, this restriction in relation to the 'decisional materials' is itself an indication of a formalist interpretative strategy.[9]

English commercial law is often regarded by commentators working within other jurisdictions as relatively formal.[10] Sunstein and Vermeule write, 'In England, interpretation is far more rigid than in the United States ... Roughly speaking, the English lawmaking system displays active, professionalized legislative oversight and a formalist judiciary'.[11] Katz also states that '... if US parties want to have their dispute heard by a court, they cannot avoid the application of the UCC in a way that transnational litigants can opt into a more formal regime by providing for their contract to be interpreted under the laws of England and enforced by a tribunal sitting in

---

9 See Katz, A.W., 'The Economics of Form and Substance in Contract Interpretation' (2004) 104 *Col LR* 496, 516. Hereafter, 'Form and Substance'.
10 Lord Steyn, 'Does Formalism Hold Sway in England?', 58.
11 Sunstein, C. and Vermeule, A., 'Interpretation and Institutions' (2003) 101 *Mich L R* 885, 924–5.

London'.[12] The fact that interpretation problems in English law are regarded as 'one-offs', where precedents offer little assistance, may incline judges towards formalism, at least in relation to interpretative method. Thus the 'rules of construction', which now seem out of favour, look like an attempt to impose order on what might otherwise appear to be an intuitive, perhaps even creative, process. However, while English contract law might be regarded as relatively formal, given the difficulty of clearly separating 'formalism' and 'contextualism' at any given point, it can be agreed that 'The real question is "what degree of formalism?" rather than "formalist or not?" . . . The real division is along a continuum'.[13] This also recognises that formalism is not opposed to contextualism but operates within it.[14] Once that is understood, formalism need not be dismissed as a wholly negative interpretative method.

Formalism and interpretation

The centre of the debate on interpretative method may not be between formalism and contextualism, but between formalism and interpretation. In *Mannai*, for example, the minority in the House of Lords did not regard the case as necessarily concerned with interpretation at all; rather, the issue was over the validity of the tenant's notice to terminate within the formal framework of obligations set out in the contract. The contract contained the 'rules' for a valid termination of the agreement; the tenant had failed to follow them, with the result that the notice was ineffective. In the colourful imagery of Lord Goff, 'The simple fact is that the tenant has failed to use the right key which alone is capable of turning the lock'.[15] For Lord Goff and Lord Jauncey, the case turned on whether the formal requirements set out in the agreement had been satisfied. In contrast, for the majority of the House of Lords, the dispute centred on interpretation. The main authority on which the minority based their decision, Lord Greene's judgment in *Hankey v Clavering*,[16] was

---

12 Katz, A.W., 'The Relative Costs of Incorporating Trade Usage into Domestic versus International Sales Contracts' (2004) 5 *Chi J Int'l L* 181, 187.
13 Sunstein, 'Must Formalism be Defended Empirically?', 640. See, also, Katz, 'Form and Substance', 505.
14 See Smith, *Contract Theory*, 276.
15 [1997] 3 All ER 352, 355.
16 [1942] 2 KB 326.

denounced by Lord Steyn as 'rigid and formalistic'. By regarding the problem as one concerning interpretation, the majority were able to use a more flexible technique to override the formal requirements for termination that the parties had agreed in the documents.

In many cases satisfying the requirements of form is important – either to signify to the parties the seriousness of their undertaking, or to combat fraud. In such cases, the importance of observing the correct formalities may make the documents impervious to inter-pretation – near enough is not good enough. However, it may be difficult to predict when strict compliance with formalities will be required, and when formalities will be relaxed through a process of interpretation. An interesting contrast with *Mannai* is the later Court of Appeal decision in *Fernandez v McDonald*.[17] The facts were very similar to *Mannai*. A landlord sought to recover possession of a property from his tenants. The tenants occupied the property under a statutory periodic tenancy, which ran from the fourth of one month to the third of the next month. The relevant requirements for the landlord's notice were found in s 21(4) of the Housing Act 1988. This section required a notice to the tenant in writing 'stating that, after a date specified in the notice, being the last day of a period of the tenancy and not earlier than two months after the date the notice was given, possession of the dwelling house is required'. The land-lord's notice stated that he required possession on 4 January, but he did not specify the last day of the tenancy (3 January). Was this a valid notice for the purposes of s 21(4)? The Court of Appeal, over-turning the first instance judge, held that it was not. Noting the large volume of possession proceedings in the County Court, Hale LJ remarked, 'it matters less which way the issue is resolved than that it is resolved one way or the other'.[18] The need for certainty and con-sistency was apparent. As a matter of interpretation, the case looks indistinguishable from *Mannai*: if the reasonable recipient could understand the message conveyed by notice, the notice ought to be valid to achieve its purpose.[19] But the Court of Appeal regarded this as the wrong test to apply. Their approach was to identify the statutory requirements and assess whether they had been complied with. Since the statute required the notice to state the last day of

17 [2004] 1 WLR 1027.
18 Ibid., at [6].
19 See, also, the decision in *Peer Freeholds Ltd v Clean Wash International Ltd* [2005] EWHC 179 (ChD).

the tenancy, and not the date when the landlord required possession, it was invalid under the statute. The parallels with the minority approach in *Mannai* are obvious and it might be wondered why *Fernandez* is categorised as concerned with form, rather than interpretation.

One answer might be that statutory schemes specifying notice requirements should be more rigidly construed than similar contractual schemes that are agreed between the parties as part of a private arrangement. Contracts do not have the same authority over the parties as binding rules of law. Hence, while statutory requirements must be strictly complied with, private agreements between the parties can be more flexibly interpreted. The Housing Act is underpinned by policy considerations concerning the balance of interests between landlords and tenants of residential property where there is no security of tenure. The Court of Appeal pointed out that it was an area where certainty was crucial, and it was relatively easy for the landlord to comply ('a defective notice can be cured the same day'[20]). This differed from the position with a commercial lease entered into on a contractual basis, which offered a much more restricted opportunity to terminate by way of a 'break clause' and which meant the tenant could be locked into paying higher than market rent for some considerable time. Nevertheless, although the reasonable landlord in *Mannai*, fully apprised of the relevant context, would have understood the tenant's meaning by the defective notice, the 'real landlord' was surely still justified in arguing that that was not what had been agreed. The comparison between these cases shows how case classification is important. *Mannai* was a case about *interpretation and meaning*, and not *form* (the majority noted that the notice was not required to be given in any particular form) whereas *Fernandez* was treated as the reverse.

The fact that cases may be classified as raising issues of interpretation, rather than form, demonstrates the potential for interpretation to engulf much judicial reasoning about contracts and contract law. This, in turn, tends to obscure that an important element of judicial *choice* is involved. A reliance on the documents, and the belief that they should be interpreted relatively strictly, with limited reference to contextual material, would seem to involve an interpretative choice, which is informed by the judges' view of both their role

20 [2004] 1 WLR 1027 at [23].

and how the dispute should be resolved. Thus questions of interpretation and construction give judges room for exercising discretion and power, both in relation to what they regard as an interpretative problem and how the interpretation should be undertaken. The choice of interpretative strategy is partly an issue about authority between the parties and the courts.[21] *Mannai* is a good illustration of how contextual interpretation can be used to interfere with private contractual arrangements. Upholding the contractual arrangement may be dismissed as 'formalistic', but by treating the case as concerning interpretation, the majority is better able to manipulate the parties' obligations, based on considerations of reasonableness. The minority in *Mannai*, in treating the dispute as concerned with form did at least show deference to the contractual scheme agreed to by the parties. *Fernandez* similarly illustrates that there are circumstances where the requirements of form will not be overridden by contextual interpretation. It is not suggested here that *Mannai* is incorrectly decided (as a matter of interpretation it most likely is correctly decided); rather the concern is whether the parties themselves may have a preference for form over substance in contract interpretation, and how they might exercise greater control over the interpretation techniques applied to their agreement.

Should formalism be taken seriously?

If one reason for adopting a contextual approach to interpretation is to allow courts better access to the social underpinnings of the agreement, or the 'reasonable expectations' of the contractors, is it conceivable that some parties might prefer a more formal method? The US literature on contracts has seen something of a countertrend emerging against contextualism in contracts interpretation, called neoformalism or 'anti-anti-formalism'.[22] Some of this literature is

---

21 Stoljar, N., 'Interpretation, Indeterminacy and Authority: Some Recent Controversies in the Philosophy of Law' (2003) 11 *J Pol Phil* 470, 470.

22 Charny, D., 'The New Formalism in Contract' (1999) 66 *U Chi L R* 842 at 842 (referring to 'anti-anti-formalism'); op. cit., Ben-Shahar; Epstein, R., 'Confusion about Custom: Disentangling Informal Customs from Standard Contractual Provisions' (1999) 66 *U Chi L R* 821; Scott, R.E., 'The Case for Formalism in Relational Contract' (2000) 94 *Northwestern Uni L R* 847; Woodward, W., 'Neoformalism in a Real World of Forms' (2001) *Wis L R* 971; Murray, J., 'Contract Theories and the Rise of Neoformalism' (2002) 71 *Fordham L R* 869; Hunter, H., 'The Growing Uncertainty about Good Faith in American Contract Law' (2002)

based on empirical studies detailing the private and formalistic dispute resolution procedures that exist in particular industries. Some commentators regard this as evidence of a commercial revolt against the flexible modes of interpretation sanctioned by instruments such as the Uniform Commercial Code. For example, article 1–303(d) of the UCC states that:

> A course of performance or course of dealing between the parties or usage of trade in the vocation or trade in which they are engaged or of which they are or should be aware is relevant in ascertaining the meaning of the parties' agreement, may give particular meaning to specific terms of the agreement, and may supplement or qualify the terms of the agreement. A usage of trade applicable in the place in which part of the performance under the agreement is to occur may be so utilized as to that part of the performance.

Much of the neoformalist agenda is rooted in the tradition of law and economics, where the predominant concerns are reducing the costs of the contracting process and promoting economically efficient outcomes. Scholars sympathetic to this tradition also express a concern that power be revested in the contracting parties, allowing them the freedom to set their own terms, which are interpreted strictly according to a parol evidence rule.[23] Many neoformalists regard their position as compatible with contextualism, arguing that their concern is with the organisation and structure of contract *law*, rather than contract as a social institution.[24] As has been seen, the relationship between the social and the legal aspects of contracting is difficult, but, in so far as the law of contract professes itself concerned with supporting market transactions, it must be concerned with implementing the kind of regime that transactors want. In this

---

20 *J of Contract Law* 31; Bernstein, L., 'Merchant Law in a Merchant Court: Rethinking the Code's Search for Immanent Business Norms' (1996) 144 *Uni Pennsylvania L R* 1765 (hereafter 'Merchant Law'), 'The Questionable Empirical Basis of Article 2's Incorporation Strategy: A Preliminary Study' (1999) 66 *Uni Chi L R* 710 (hereafter 'Empirical Basis') and 'Private Commercial Law in the Cotton Industry: Creating Co-operation Through Rules, Norms and Institutions' (2001) 99 *Mich L R* 1724 (hereafter 'Cotton Industry').

23 Op. cit., Scott, at 866.
24 Scott, R.E., 'The Death of Contract Law' (2004) 54 *Univ of Toronto L J* 369, 370.

respect, both more formal and more contextual approaches may have a role, depending on the contractual circumstances. In other words, English law need not give up its developing individualistic, flexible and contextual approach, provided it is sensitive to the fact that some contractors may require a stricter method.

Neoformalism: theoretical or empirical?

Traditionally, formalism (or adopting a textualist, or literalist, approach to the contractual documents) has been defended on 'principled' grounds. MacCormick has written that 'it has to be recognised that behind what are often described somewhat disapprovingly as "formalistic" or "legalistic" approaches to interpretation there do lie evaluative reasons of a highly respectable kind'.[25] Such arguments are perhaps more familiar in the sphere of statutory interpretation than contractual interpretation. In the former, a formalistic plain meaning strategy is justified by appealing to democratic values of the rule of law and the separation of powers.[26] In relation to neoformalism, two related things are apparent. The first is the way in which the new formalism is justified largely on either empirical or pragmatic grounds, rather than on grounds of theory or principle. To the extent that the formalist sympathiser can demonstrate that formalism is an interpretative strategy that some contracting parties might choose, they should be taken seriously. The second is the way in which formalism can be understood not as opposed to contextualism, but as a position within contextualism. In the remainder of this chapter, both theoretical and empirical formalism will be examined. The question of how formalism may fit within 'relational' contract theory will be explored, together with some of the reasons why parties might prefer a more formal interpretative approach to be taken to their contracts. The next chapter will consider how the parties, through contractual methods, might influence the interpretative method applied to their agreement.

Empirically defended formalism

Modern versions of formalism in contract rely on empiricism to substantiate their claims. It would perhaps be more accurate to say

25 MacCormick, *Rhetoric and the Rule of Law*, 127.
26 Op. cit., Stoljar, 482.

that commentators on formalism have *recognised* that neoformalism must be justified on the basis of empirical evidence. However, they have not necessarily been concerned with providing that evidence. One exception to this is Lisa Bernstein, whose work is discussed below. Other, law and economics, scholars have relied on 'rational behaviour' models to make their point. Despite the lack of hard evidence, the *idea* of empirical formalism has won some support. Sunstein argues that neoformalism, in so far as it is defended along empirical or realist lines, is much stronger than 'old style' formalism that was defended by conceptual arguments concerning legitimacy or authority. He states that 'a good defence of formalism must be empirical', that is 'it must depend upon factual assumptions and claims'.[27] He goes on to hypothesise that 'it is disagreement over the underlying empirical issues – not over large concepts of any kind [e.g. legitimacy ... or separation of powers] that principally separates formalists and non-formalists'.[28] Katz has written that neoformalism 'attempts to ground formalism in functional terms; it tries to show how formal methods of interpretation help to forward practical goals such as efficiency, procedural fairness and public accountability'.[29] More generally, Kaplow has argued that the choice between rules and standards in legal regulation of activities depends upon the interplay of various factors that can only be verified by empirical, or factual, study.[30] One of the possible factual disputes is how much reliance should be placed on the contractual documents as an accurate statement of the parties' obligations and how far the parties intended the documents to constitute the regulatory framework of the agreement.

Some empirical evidence supportive of increased formalism in commercial law exists in the work of US scholar Lisa Bernstein. In three very influential studies, she undertook empirical work into dispute resolution procedures in various industries and commodity markets.[31] Her findings appear to challenge the UCC approach of directing the application of 'immanent business norms' to issues of contracts interpretation and dispute resolution.[32] In her examinations

27 Sunstein, 'Must Formalism be Defended Empirically?', 641.
28 Ibid., Sunstein, 642.
29 Katz, 'Form and Substance', 497.
30 Kaplow, L., 'Rules versus Standards: An Economic Analysis' (1992) 42 *Duke L J* 557, 563.
31 Op. cit., Bernstein.
32 Bernstein, 'Merchant Law', 1768.

of private dispute resolution procedures within certain industries,
she found that arbitrators adhered rigidly to the stated rules of the
trade association within which the contractors did business. In particular, the arbitrators saw their first task as enforcing the terms of
the contract, using trade rules when terms did not yield an answer,
and only then trade customs.[33] This suggests that some contractors,
in some circumstances, prefer a more formalistic approach to be
taken. Bernstein's work is discussed in more detail at various points
below, where possible reasons for the preference for formalism are
examined. This emphasis on empiricism has shifted the focus of
formalism away from grand claims about legitimacy, towards eluci-
dating the pragmatic considerations that may incline contractors
to favour a formal interpretative regime over a substantive one.[34]
Such arguments may provide a justification for limiting recourse to
contextual material, rather than expanding it.

Theoretically defended formalism

Apart from the empirical and pragmatic considerations, attempts to
defend formalism can also be made on theoretical or principled
grounds. Such lines of argument require consideration of difficult
conceptual issues concerning legitimacy, authority and the judicial
role. While contract enforcement and dispute resolution do not generally raise issues of broad democratic principle, they do raise issues
concerning the respective roles of the contracting parties and the
court. The judicial role is often said to be to uphold the bargain the
parties have made, not to create a new one. While such statements
can be dismissed as rhetoric, the idea of the protection of party
autonomy continues to exert influence in contract law and formalism
does defer to this concern. This makes formalism attractive to some
scholars. For example Schauer argues that formalism is essentially
about the balance of power and the denial of discretion.[35] He writes,
'Part of what formalism is about is its inculcation of the view that
sometimes it is appropriate for decisionmakers to recognize their
lack of jurisdiction and to defer even when they are convinced that
their own judgment is best'.[36] Sunstein also supports the view that

33 Ibid., 1777.
34 See, generally, Katz, 'Form and Substance'.
35 Op cit., Woodward, 974.
36 Ibid., Schauer, 543–4.

interpretative method is concerned with power. He remarks, 'People trying to choose an interpretative method must decide how to allocate power among various groups and institutions – indeed, allocating power is what the choice of an interpretive method *does*'.[37] Once this is appreciated, one of the questions in relation to interpretation would be whether '*the parties* have withdrawn from the court the power or opportunity to give a purposive interpretation of their agreement'.[38]

According to this line of scholarship then, one important contextual inquiry in contract interpretation is as to the interpretative method the parties wanted applied to their contract. So, for example, '[w]hether, and to what extent, a court is to consider the document integrated ought to depend in the first instance on how the *parties* intended the court to go about its interpretive job'.[39] Such enquiries would be 'contextual' since the search would be for evidence that suggested the parties want a more formal, or less formal and more contextual, approach to their agreement. The answer to the question of whether parties would prefer a more or less formal approach will vary between parties and contractual circumstances, but there is no reason to think this evidential search is any more onerous or indeterminate than that currently required by contextual interpretation. What empirical evidence there is suggests that contracting parties care little for the regime and rules of contract law. In that case it may not much matter what interpretative regime the courts adopt, provided the parties know what it is and can opt-out accordingly. In these circumstances, only some prima facie case can be advanced about why formalism should be taken seriously as an interpretative theory that the parties might choose, and the circumstances in which they would choose it. The important point to grasp is that courts must have a variety of interpretative strategies at their disposal and, crucially, strategies for determining which kind of interpretative technique is appropriate. There are a variety of considerations that would incline the courts to one interpretative method rather than another. This is perhaps the real relevance of context – in suggesting interpretative approaches, rather than concrete outcomes. A court's intellectual and justificatory energies may be better spent addressing

37 Sunstein, C., *Legal Reasoning and Political Conflict*, 168–9 (emphasis in original).
38 Op. cit., Woodward, 975 (emphasis in original).
39 Ibid., Woodward, 977 (emphasis in original).

this issue, rather than concentrating all their efforts on the contextual meaning of words of the contractual text.

Formalism and relational contract

Formalism (and literalism), if it is to have any role, must be a strategy that takes place within a broadly contextual approach. But isn't formalism the antithesis of contextualism and isn't contextualism designed to try and bridge the gap between the social and legal elements of contract regulation, to bring law back into line with life? As has already been discussed, the movement towards contextualism in contract is closely connected with, if not indistinguishable from, the view that contracts are, first and foremost, social phenomena. A writer particularly associated with this view of contract is Ian Macneil. It is not possible to deal with all the elements of his essential contract theory in a few short paragraphs, or to do it justice, but his theory may help us to understand why formalism might be compatible with contextualism.

To the extent that Macneil's position is that no contracting or exchange behaviour can be divorced from context (however broadly defined) – all contracting is relational[40] – this suggests that formalism is an attempt to achieve the impossible: to understand the contractual relationship without reference to the social context at all. The fact that the parties have attempted to formulate a complete statement of their obligations, and all the terms and conditions that will govern their relationship, cannot thereby wipe out the co-operative aspects of their agreement. Nevertheless, the parties might choose formality in an attempt to impose the qualities that Macneil calls 'presentation' and 'discreteness' on the deal. Presentation is 'a rendering of past and particularly future events or structures influencing present allocative decisions as if they were present'[41] or bringing the future effectively into the present,[42] while 'discreteness is the separating of a transaction from all else between the participants at

---

40 It seems that Macneil should no longer be associated with the popular view that there is a spectrum of contract types, with wholly discrete contracts at one end and relational contracts at the other: see, Campbell, D. ch 1, in Macneil, I., *The Relational Theory of Contract: Selected Works of Ian Macneil* (ed. D. Campbell), 2001, London: Sweet and Maxwell, at 5 and 20–1.

41 Ibid., Campbell, 39.

42 Ibid., Macneil, 182.

the same time and before and after'.[43] Attempts at complete presentiation will fail because of lack of relevant information: 'Bounded
rationality obviously makes presentation an illusory goal. Given
relevant information shortcomings, contracts will be incomplete'.[44]
Information gathering is costly, and 'under these circumstances,
contracts of a more complex character are characterised by their
provision for flexibility in the obligations undertaken'.[45]

Despite this, it would be too crude to regard formalism as an
insignificant attempt to do the impossible under Macneil's theory.
This is not least because 'Macneil's relational approach and a law-
and-society perspective do not offer elegant models of contracting
behavior. You get a story and multiple factors to consider, but not
a simple formula that produces results.'[46] Macneil's theory is an
attempt to explain *all manner* of contracting behaviour and to this
end, at least as important as the relational/discrete distinction, if not
the core of his relational theory, is his elucidation of the common
contract norms – the essential elements of contract behaviour that
are present in all contracts.[47] It is not possible to consider in detail
the operation of all the norms here. What is important to note is that
it is possible for contracts to be *more or less* relational, or *more or less*
discrete depending on the operation and interaction of the norms. If
parties want discreteness they simply 'enhance' some norms at the
expense of others. Macneil writes, 'While all the contract norms
operate in the behaviour and in the internal principles and rules of
all kinds of contract, some assume special importance in discrete
transactions and others assume special importance in contractual
relations.'[48] Within the scheme of the common contract norms, the
idea of the discrete exchange is not irrelevant or a misconception. It
only becomes a misconception if it is regarded as existing in isol-
ation, rather than as part of contractual agreements and exchanges

43 Ibid., Macneil, 154.
44 Campbell, D., 'The Relational Constitution of Contract and the Limits of
    "Economics": Kenneth Arrow on the Social Background of Markets' in S. Deakin
    and J. Michie (eds), *Contracts, Co-operation and Competition*, 1997, Oxford: OUP,
    307 at 313.
45 Ibid., at 314.
46 Macaulay, S., 'Relational Contracts Floating On A Sea Of Custom? Thoughts
    About The Ideas Of Ian Macneil and Lisa Bernstein' (2000) 94 *Northwestern Univ
    L Rev* 775, 783.
47 Op. cit., Macneil, 152–67.
48 Op. cit., Macneil, 154.

that are *always* relational. Although it is artificial, the parties may choose discreteness. Campbell writes, 'Given that even discrete contract rests on the common norms, the possibility of treating an exchange as discrete can "properly arise only after a recognition that a decision is being made to treat the pertinent aspect of exchange relations as if it were discrete, although in fact it is not, in short to ignore the non-discrete aspect of the relation"'.[49] Indeed, Macneil postulates the existence of the 'discrete norm', which is the product of two other norms: effectuation of consent and implementation of planning. Implementation of planning is 'the attempt closely to specify (and impose strict liability for) performance'.[50] Macneil goes on to say, 'the closer the parties are to behaving and governing themselves in accordance with this discrete norm, the more they will choose planning that is completely binding (or as close to completely binding as they can get), thereby bringing the future into the present as much as is humanly possible.'[51]

There would appear to be nothing in Macneil's theory that denies that the parties might want at least some aspects of their contractual relationship to be governed by the discrete norm. The parties may therefore choose mechanisms that attempt to impose discreteness on the relationship, presumably because the parties see some advantage in doing so – in Macneil's view, when the parties want precision and focus in their contractual dealings.[52] So, for example, the parties might try to specify in advance as many of the obligations as possible and may prefer a formalistic interpretative approach to be taken to the agreement. But this decision to emphasise the discrete norm is not without sacrifice. The parties sacrifice the relational values that come from the relational norms such as 'preservation of the relation and harmonization of relational contract'.[53] In relation to the discrete transaction, Macneil writes, '[f]lexibility is achieved, not within the discrete transaction, where all is rigid presentation, but outside it, in the repeated use of numerous discrete transactions. Contractual solidarity is maintained only through external forces, such as the law

49 Op. cit., Campbell, 23, quoting I. Macneil, 'Relational Contract Theory as Sociology: A Reply to Professors Lindenberg and de Vos' (1987) 143 *J. of Institutional and Theoretical Economics* 272, 277.
50 Ibid., Campbell, 21.
51 Op. cit., Macneil, 154–5.
52 Ibid., 158.
53 Ibid., 161.

of contract, implementing the presentiated discrete transaction.'[54] The loss that is involved here is well expressed by Charny, 'negotiating a legally enforceable contract . . . may create anxiety by making the parties conscious of the risks of breach. Negotiation may also create or intensify an adversarial atmosphere by raising the specter of litigation for transactors who wish to view themselves as friends or partners.'[55] Nevertheless, the conclusion is that, 'There is nothing in relational contract theory that should cause its adherents to reject formalist contract doctrine in all circumstances.'[56] The question that arises now is how and why the parties might want to exclude the relational, or contextual, aspects of their agreement from the judge's consideration. The following section considers this issue.

Why might the parties choose formalism?

There are a variety of reasons why parties may want to limit the available information about the contractual relationship to the documents, and require the courts to place a strict interpretation on those documents. In other words, there are cogent reasons why, in some circumstances, formalism should be taken seriously as the interpretative theory to be applied.

The costs of contextualism

The first and most obvious reason for confining a court's enquiry to the four corners of the agreement relates to the possible costs involved in the contextual approach.[57] It has been noted that this has been a particular concern of some judges. Two particular kinds of cost are pertinent: transaction costs (broadly, the costs of reaching and recording the deal)[58] and enforcement costs (broadly, the costs of ensuring compliance and resolving disputes).[59] One of the arguments

54 Ibid., 162.
55 Charny, D., 'Non-legal Sanctions in Commercial Relationships' (1990) 104 *Harv L R* 375, 407.
56 Whitford, W., 'Relational Contracts and the New Formalism' (2004) *Wis L R* 631, 635.
57 Scott, 'The Case for Formalism', at 874; Posner, E., 'The Parol Evidence Rule, the Plain Meaning Rule and the Principles of Contractual Interpretation' (1998) 146 *Uni Pennsylvania L R* 533, 540–1.
58 See, general discussion, in Scott, 'The Case for Formalism', at 862ff.
59 See, generally, Charny, 'Non-legal Sanctions', 405ff.

in favour of contextualism over literalism is that it lowers transaction costs, since it relieves the parties of having to reduce all the terms and standards that govern the agreement to writing in the final document.[60] Parties can write a simpler document, leaving it to the courts to fill gaps through the process of contextual interpretation. In relation to writing, parties face particular difficulties over terms that relate to perceived remote risks (where the costs of reaching an agreement on the matter are high relative to the benefits of reaching agreement) or in what are expected to be long-term business relationships, where flexibility is required and renegotiation expected to make the contract work,[61] or where accurate information is lacking or is too costly to obtain. If litigation occurs the court can utilise contextual material such as previous deals, customs of the trade, the common understandings of the parties, open-textured standards such as reasonableness and good faith or the applicable default rules.[62] The argument is that the more expansive the court's interpretative approach, the less specific the parties have to be in the written terms of their agreement.

The transaction cost argument does not provide any independent support for the contextual approach: one can only place confidence in contextual interpretation to lower transaction costs if that approach is already in place and the parties have broad confidence that the outcomes would reflect what would have been bargained for. In other words, the parties' (or their lawyers') trust in the courts to reach the right result must come first. The level of trust parties place in the courts will, of course, vary between different kinds of contractor and contracting situation. The difficulty is that relying on the court's gap-filling function may reduce transaction costs, but at the expense of increasing enforcement costs if and when disputes arise, even if many of the costs of administering the courts system are sunk or borne by others.[63] Of course, contracting parties may prefer reduced transaction costs since 'contracting costs are incurred today with certainty while dispute resolution costs are incurred tomorrow

60 Kraus, J. and Walt, S., 'In Defense of The Incorporation Strategy' in J. Kraus and S. Walt (eds), *The Jurisprudential Foundations of Corporate and Commercial Law*, 2000, Cambridge: CUP, 193 at 200. Collins, *Regulating Contracts*, 177–8.
61 Ibid., Collins, at 163.
62 Ibid., Collins, at 181.
63 Charny, 'Non-legal Sanctions', 405

and probabilistically'.[64] Litigation may be regarded as a remote con-
tingency, the costs of preparing for which do not appear worth it at
the agreement phase. Nevertheless, if litigation results where substantial 'gap filling' is required, this may add significantly to the
costs. This is because the relevant 'context' has to be established.
Expert testimony may have to be adduced, preliminary hearings may
be required on matters of evidence and procedure and so on.[65] There
is no guarantee that this additional evidence would change the outcome a judge would reach on consideration of a much more limited
range of evidence.[66] Higher 'interpretive error costs'[67] are also a risk –
in seeking to establish the relevant context, the courts may make mistakes; the greater the amount of contextual material, the greater the
possibility for error. Decision-makers may easily become 'bewildered
by a large set of conflicting evidence'.[68]

Contextualist interpretation then may place a large verification
burden on the courts. In view of this, it is not wholly unreasonable
that some commercial parties may incur increased transaction costs,
and attempt a greater degree of planning and formality, in the hope
of reducing enforcement costs. Of course, whether they choose to do
this depends on a number of variable factors which, in the end, can
probably only be established by empirical evidence. Courts would
have to assess this on a case-by-case basis. One can only hypothesise
about the kinds of circumstances where the parties might make this
choice: new contracting partners with whom trust is not yet established, areas of developing technology with high failure rates, high
risk or unusual ventures with a greater likelihood of disputes, and so
on.[69] The availability of in-house lawyers to draft such agreements
may also have an important effect. Repeat contractors may be
encouraged to bear these increased costs with the hope of incurring
them once only, but then being able to use the resulting terms on
several occasions with different contracting partners.[70] In relation to

64 Schwartz, A. and Scott, R.E., 'Contract Theory and the Limits of Contract Law'
(2003) 113 *Yale L J* 541, 585.
65 McKendrick, 'Lord Hoffmann's Restatement', 147.
66 Vermeule, A., 'Three Strategies of Interpretation' (2005) 42 *San Diego L R* 607, 614.
67 Op. cit., Kraus and Walt, 193.
68 Vermeule, 'Three Strategies of Interpretation', 614.
69 Cunningham, L., 'Toward A Prudential and Credibility-Centered Parol Evidence
Rule' (2000) 68 *Uni Cincinnati L R* 269, 274; Beale and Dugdale, 'Planning and
Use of Contractual Remedies', 48; Katz, 'Form and Substance', 536.
70 Charny, 'Non-legal Sanctions', 436–7.

some commercial contracts it is perhaps more natural for the parties to want a formalistic approach if their contract is detailed and seemingly complete, particularly if the parties have been advised by lawyers, are of equal bargaining power and repeat contractors in the market. Such considerations might explain the relative formalism of the *Total Gas Marketing v Arco British* decision for example. Of course the impossibility of complete presentiation is still a formidable obstacle. Nevertheless, contractual means are available by which parties can deal with changes in circumstances – price variation clauses, mechanisms to extend time for performance, and so on, although it must be admitted that these require some advance planning and foresight. In relation to this it has been noted that:

> it is wholly incorrect to claim that knowledgeable parties who are closeted together for years can anticipate and correct only an 'infinitesimal fraction' of their relevant business problems. The problem with botched transactions has to do with haste, and not with the power of language. The provision of standard term agreements reduces these pressures by allowing parties to make important trades on a moment's notice precisely because standard packages are available to facilitate them. . . . The real challenge to these standard contract provisions rests . . . not on their indeterminacy, but on their substantive fairness.[71]

Whitford points out the danger, however – that parties haggling over terms at the formation stage lose sight of central concerns: 'Negotiations about specific contract terms can take the focus away from what is most important at this time – performance planning within each firm and building trust between firms.'[72] But this must be a sacrifice that it is up to the parties to make.

---

71 Epstein, 'Confusion about Custom', 828. That commercial parties might have more input into written contracts than is sometimes assumed is borne out by the recent case of *George Wimpey UK Ltd v V I Construction Ltd*, [2005] EWCA Civ 77. The parties to a contract for the sale of land for residential development included a formula in the contract for determining base purchase price plus overage depending on actual sale prices of the flats. The lawyers disclaimed responsibility for the formula, writing that they did not understand it and therefore could not advise on it: para [16]. Clearly the extent of the businessman's, as opposed to the lawyer's, input into the contract will vary. Macaulay writes, 'sometimes, writings labeled "contract" do capture many if not most of the expectations of those who sign them', 'Real Deal', 51.
72 Op. cit., Whitford, 637.

A related problem is that litigation over terms and obligations is actually *encouraged* (and hence costs incurred) by courts adopting a contextual approach, both in relation to terms and the initial issue of whether a contract even exists. It has been argued that the move to standards increases enforcement costs for contracting parties because of their unpredictability and lack of transparency.[73] One can readily think of examples where one party's case is built upon 'context' rather than a strict application of contract doctrines. The decision in *Williams v Roffey*[74] demonstrates an appreciation of the parties' understandings and the context of their agreement, but there are also numerous counterexamples. One of these is *Carlton and Granada v The Football League.*[75] Here, the defendant entered into an agreement with a subsidiary company of the claimants, believing the financial obligations of the subsidiary to be guaranteed by the claimants. Evidence of the social context of the parties' relationship demonstrated the extent to which both parties understood that the success of the arrangement depended upon the support and co-operation of the claimants, but in the end the defendants were not able to make out the legal case that the formal requirements for a guarantee had been satisfied. The case was therefore disposed of by a relatively straightforward application of the classical contract law rules concerning agency, the Statute of Frauds 1677 and the phrase 'subject to contract'. One wonders how far the litigation in that case was encouraged by courts' progressive relaxation of the contract rules. For such litigants, the mix between the application of classical law with occasional unpredictable departures that attempt to give effect to the 'context of the agreement' or the 'reasonable expect-ations of the parties' may look like the worst of both worlds. In this situation it is more understandable that the parties will attempt to take control of interpretative method, or resort to other dispute reso-lution mechanisms. As Scott has put it, 'many contracting parties have chosen to exit the public system of legal enforcement in favour of less costly alternatives over which they have more control'.[76] He regards the move from bright line rules to vague standards and

---

73 Scott, 'Death of Contract Law', 374.
74 [1991] 1 QB 1.
75 [2002] EWHC 1650. See, also, *Baird v Marks and Spencer* [2001] EWCA Civ 274; [2002] 1 All ER (Comm) 737.
76 Scott, 'Death of Contract Law', 370.

contextualist interpretation as responsible for the 'exodus of contracting parties' from contract law.[77]

A further problem is that much reliance on context may be done strategically – the problem of 'threshing through the undergrowth'[78] for the chance remark upon which to build a case. The suspicion is often raised of the strategic reliance on context to sanction an escape from a bad bargain.[79] While the reverse is also true, and a party may strategically seek an advantage by relying on the strict words of a contract while knowing that the documents did not reflect the parties' joint understanding, the contextual approach is arguably more open to this kind of strategic abuse, given the range of evidence that it is possible to adduce under the label of 'matrix of fact'. The weakness of the written contract here is its incompleteness. One may use the 'context' to seek an unbargained for advantage in imposing terms after the parties are in a contractual relationship, even in circumstances where the written terms appear relatively complete.[80]

There are also problems relating to 'agency'. Commercial contracts are negotiated by representatives and employees, but may be entered into by different entities, usually companies.[81] This consideration may prompt the 'contractor' to attempt greater formality and planning in the documents, and to require a strict interpretation of the contract. This is for two main reasons. The first is to ensure that the things that their employees and representatives have said and done during negotiations do not bind the company. Much depends here on how much trust firms have in their negotiators and representatives, and how much control they exercise over them.[82] The second is that of creating accurate records of the transaction that can be relied upon by its implementers. Berg writes:

> . . . if two companies enter into a complicated transaction, one of the main purposes in instructing lawyers to draft the contract is to ensure that its terms will be clear to those who have to deal

77 Ibid., Scott, at 370–7.
78 Per Lightman J, *The Inntrepreneur Pub Co v East Crown Ltd* (ChD) [2000] 3 EGLR 31 at [7].
79 Op. cit., Schwartz and Scott, 585–6.
80 In relation to strategic behaviour, see Campbell, 'The Relational Constitution of Contract', 312–13.
81 See, generally, Katz, 'Form and Substance', 532–4.
82 Ibid., Katz, 533–4.

with the contract in the future, and to the lawyers advising them, after the management who negotiated the contract have retired or moved on. The contract is therefore drafted so that it can be used by – it is addressed to – people who will have little of the background knowledge of the original management.[83]

As far as courts are concerned, these sorts of consideration might prompt a preference for documents over more unreliable evidence given by negotiators, representatives and employees. These difficulties are considered further below.

Judicial error

Judges may make mistakes over the significance of the contextual material to the parties' agreement. Sunstein writes:

> In the law of contract, an error can be defined as an outcome different from what the parties would have chosen if they had made explicit provision on the point . . . Courts that do not care about what the parties would have done, and that look instead to the objective meaning of contractual terms, should be taken to be saying that this method of interpretation is most likely to minimize decision costs and error costs.[84]

Error, then, might be found in producing outcomes at the litigation stage, which the parties would not have agreed to if they had been asked at the formation stage. This might occur if the courts enforced some extracontractual statement the parties did not want enforced, or interpreted the contract in a way that was counter to the parties' intentions. Whether formalist or nonformalist judges will produce more errors depends on empirical evidence. Some care needs to be taken with the points about error, since the reality is that a court may have to make a decision on matters that the parties had not considered and over which they had no intentions. This makes it difficult to assess whether an error has in fact occurred. Nevertheless, there

---

83 Berg, A., 'Thrashing Through the Undergrowth' (2006) 122 *LQR* 354, 359.
84 'Must Formalism be Defended Empirically?', 648. See, also, Posner, E., 'Parol Evidence Rule', 542–3; Posner, E., 'A Theory Of Contract Law Under Conditions Of Radical Judicial Error' (2000) 94 *Nw U L R* 749 (hereafter 'Error'); op. cit., Schwartz and Scott, 587.

are some general points to be made. The contextual approach arguably increases the chances for error by increasing the amount of
information deemed relevant to the interpretation exercise. Judges
may have to deal with a significant amount of contextual material,
some of it connected to particular frameworks of analysis whose
conventions will be unfamiliar to them. In the competition law case
of *Crehan v Inntrepreneur Pub Company*, for example, economists,
accountants, valuers, surveyors and investment analysts provided
expert evidence of context.[85] It must be acknowledged that the courts
could err in dealing with this sort of evidence.[86] There is no guarantee that contextualism will produce error-free decision-making. Of
course the reverse is also true, and formalism may produce errors,
but this kind of error is easier for the parties to predict and take steps
to avoid – particularly if they know the interpretation rules the
courts will generally apply.[87] In *Fulton Motors Ltd v Toyota (GB)
Ltd*[88] a car dealership and car manufacturer entered into a printed
form of agreement that specified that the contract could be terminated on giving two years notice. In fact, the parties had agreed that
the contract between them was to terminate after one year. Toyota
put the correct notice provision in a letter that accompanied the
written contract. Toyota's lawyer believed there was no need to alter
the written agreement since the letter made the true position clear.
He evidently put some confidence in a court to recognise that the
formal contract did not reflect the intentions of the parties. His confidence was not misplaced. The court concluded the letter contained
the correct notice provision, and, since it was contemporaneous with
the contract, it was also a contractual document. This conclusion
reflected the clear intentions of the parties consistent with the other
evidence.

The argument about error is related to the particular characteristics of law and, in particular, private law reasoning. Weinrib puts
the point succinctly: 'Private law . . . is more than the sum of its
results. It also includes a set of concepts, a distinctive institutional

85 [2004] EWCA 637 at [53].
86 Posner, 'Error', 753. Gava, J. and Greene, J. also recognise this problem: 'Do
   We Need a Hybrid Law of Contract?: Why Hugh Collins is Wrong and Why it
   Matters' (2004) 63 *CLJ* 605, 616–20.
87 Posner, 'Error', 752; Bernstein, 'Merchant Law', 1790, 1795; Sunstein, 'Must
   Formalism be Defended Empirically?', 647.
88 CA, unreported, 23 July 1999.

setting, and a characteristic mode of reasoning'.[89] The 'institutional setting' and 'mode of reasoning' undoubtedly gives rise to limitations in judging the context of commercial contractual agreements, particularly where that context is informed by distinctly non-legal subject-matter, such as economics.[90] A court's conclusions on the social context of a commercial agreement may be impressionistic at best, despite hearing testimony of witnesses and experts. One reason for drafting comprehensive documents is to provide a more reliable source of evidence than witnesses, who are more likely to give evidence of their states of mind and subjective intent, along with the 'context'. There is also the danger that witness evidence is self-serving and unreliable. Some judges are clearly ambivalent about the usefulness of witness evidence, preferring to rely on the documents.[91] The reliance on documents may 'restrict arbitrator discretion and minimize the need for arbitrators both to rely on and assess the credibility of testimony.'[92] Reliance on documents simplifies the interpretative task since the court is better able to place itself in the position of a reasonable recipient of the document than it is of a participant in oral negotiations and so on. Such discussions are difficult to recall accurately *ex post* within a very different context (the dispute) to that in which they were made. The difficulties judges face in forming 'an understanding of the informal conventions governing a business relation' have been well put by John Gava and Janey Greene.[93] They point out that such information is really only available to the parties themselves and that 'formalism is designed to overcome the impossibility of anyone knowing what goes on in the minds of contracting parties'.[94]

---

89 Weinrib, E., *The Idea of Private Law*, 1995, Camb., Mass: Harvard UP, 4–5.

90 Gava and Greene, 'Why Hugh Collins is Wrong', 609, on the distinction between economics, sociology and law as academic disciplines. For recent judicial appreciation of the limitations of judges in this respect see comments of Peter Gibson LJ in *Crehan v Inntrepreneur* [2004] EWCA 637 at [76].

91 See *Emcor, Drake & Scull v McAlpine* [2004] EWCA Civ 1733, at [6].

92 Bernstein, 'Merchant Law', 1819. In *Inntrepreneur v East Crown*, a witness for Inntrepreneur could not recall the details of crucial conversations he held with the defendant. The judge nevertheless described him as an 'impressive witness', at [18].

93 Op. cit., Gava and Greene, 616–20. See, also, Deakin, S. and Wilkinson, F., 'Contracts, Co-operation and Trust: The Role of the Institutional Framework' in D. Campbell and P. Vincent-Jones (eds), *Contract and Economic Organisation*, 1996, Aldershot: Dartmouth, 95 at 100–1.

94 Gava and Greene, ibid., 617. On the difficulties of judges making assessments of commercial practice and market activity see J. Gava, 'The Perils of Judicial

Error might also arise in relation to what the courts take to be an 'absurd' or 'unreasonable' result. Again, this relates to an issue about contractual power. Schauer writes, 'The question . . . is not only whether a result is absurd, but whether the decision-makers should have the jurisdiction to determine which results are absurd and which not.'[95] He continues that some regimes may 'prefer the occasional wrong or even preposterous result to a regime in which judges were empowered to search for purpose or preposterousness, for it might be that such empowerment was thought to present a risk of error or variance of decision even more harmful than the tolerance of occasional absurd results'.[96]

Flexible norms vs legal norms

Parties may prefer to have their contract governed according to its terms rather than extra-legal promises because they see value in those extra-legal promises. E. Posner makes the following remark in relation to a contextual approach to interpretation, or as he terms it, 'a soft parol evidence rule': 'By blurring the correspondence between oral representation and extra-legality, on the one hand, and the correspondence between written representation and enforceability, on the other, [a soft parol evidence rule] interferes with the use of non-legal enforcement mechanisms to maximize the value of trading relationships.'[97] This view is echoed by many writers and is also borne out by some empirical studies. Lisa Bernstein's empirical work on intratrade dispute resolution in the cotton industry reveals that many traders may opt out of the public legal system (augmenting the empirical finding that businesses may prefer not to use the law) in relation to intraindustry disputes, in favour of their own dispute resolution procedures. While the reputation of traders (rather than a contract) is essential to doing business, the dispute resolution procedures often rely on very formalistic trade rules, applied with a minimum of discretion by industry insiders.[98] The rules tend not to rely on 'open textured' standards such as good faith. Instead, bright

Activism: The Contracts Jurisprudence of Justice Michael Kirby' (1999) 15 *J Contract L* 156, 167–73.

95 Schauer, *Playing by the Rules*, 214.
96 Ibid.
97 Posner, 'The Parol Evidence Rule', 566; Scott, 'Death of Contract Law', 388.
98 Op. cit., Bernstein, 'Cotton Industry'.

line rules 'reduce the cost of entering into an agreement by providing a comprehensive set of well-tailored default rules that reduce the negotiation costs, specification costs, information costs, and relational costs of contracting, as well as the risk of transaction breakdown.'[99] She argues that a court's reliance on flexibility may actually encourage contractors to be inflexible, since they do not want to engage in a pattern of behaviour that may then cause flexibility to be imposed upon them by a court. In other words, parties want to maintain control over flexibility, they do not want it forced upon them.[100] This is echoed by Woodward, who points out that permissive rules about extrinsic evidence may actually make the parties more strict in relation to their contracts since they will not want to create any 'hostages to fortune' that hamper their future action.[101] Many writers have pointed out that legalisation may harm the development of trust between contractors and impair the effectiveness of non-legal sanctions.[102] It can be appreciated that one party's effort to be co-operative, for example by accepting late or partial delivery, or other changes to the contract, without taking steps to reserve his legal rights may be judged, according to the legal framework, to be acquiescence or as accepting a variation.

This links to a further argument concerning whether one can ensure that one's contracting partners are trustworthy and co-operative through the contract law system. Certainly parties may try with devices such as 'best endeavours' clauses, or by seeking to imply terms of co-operation.[103] However, the effectiveness of such devices has been questioned. Campbell and Harris argue that a shift in attitude must come first and without this 'formal provision for flexibility is fruitless, for one cannot create a co-operative attitude by writing down that such an attitude will be taken to contingencies as they arise'.[104] Instead, contract law acts only as background enforcement and support. It is just 'one important mechanism for dealing with

---

99 Ibid., Bernstein, 1741–2.
100 Ibid., Bernstein, 1743, 1776–7; Bernstein, 'Merchant Law', 808–9; Scott, 'Death of Contract Law', 375.
101 Woodward, 'Neoformalism', 982; op. cit., Ben-Shahar, 784.
102 Charny, 'Non-legal Sanctions', 428; Scott, 'The Case for Formalism in Relational Contract', at 852.
103 For example, by providing that a contracting partner will have 'preferred supplier status': *ProForce Recruitment Ltd v The Rugby Group* [2006] EWCA Civ 69.
104 Campbell, D. and Harris, D., 'Flexibility in Long Term Contractual Relationships: The Role of Cooperation' (1993) 20 *J. Law and Soc* 166, 173.

the essential riskiness of trust'.[105] This view about the difficulties of contracting for trust is also consistent with the view that there are, in effect, two regimes that govern any contractual relationship – the legal sanctions and the non-legal sanctions.[106] Bernstein's empirical work has again featured here. Of particular importance is the distinction she draws between the parties' use of 'relationship preserving norms' and 'endgame norms' during their agreement.[107] While during the currency of a relationship the parties may be flexible and conciliatory in an attempt to keep the commercial relationship going (employing relationship preserving norms), once the relationship breaks down (or enters the 'endgame' stage), sometimes signalled by litigation, the parties may be more willing to insist upon their legal rights and go to court to solve disputes. At the 'endgame' stage, maintaining a good relationship is no longer a priority. Collins also notes that 'the contractual framework may be invoked at any time. It will be resuscitated if the parties perceive the long term relation is about to terminate or the considerations of economic self-interest now point in the direction of strict contractual enforcement of a discrete transaction'.[108] The point is that in an 'endgame' the parties have little to gain by an application of the relationship preserving norms, which may rely more on contextual understandings.

A further point in relation to this is that very often it will not be the original contracting parties, informed of all the circumstances of the agreement and its history, but third parties – in particular, insurance companies, banks seeking to enforce securities, assignees and liquidators – that embark on commercial litigation. These sorts of parties may be more ready to stand on their legal rights and will seek enforcement according to the terms of the agreement, rather than on the basis of understandings generated between the parties. In many respects the litigation itself becomes a new context, which alters the parties' relationship and the issues in dispute. Litigation is thus an artificial point of view from which to assess the social context of the parties' agreement. For example, in *Amalgamated Investment and Property Co Ltd v Texas Commerce International Bank*, Goff J noted that there was a high degree of trust and co-operation between the

---

105 Op. cit., Deakin and Wilkinson, 112.
106 Scott, 'The Case for Formalism in Relational Contract', at 852. See, also, op. cit., Deakin and Wilkinson, 111.
107 Bernstein, 'Merchant Law', 1796ff.
108 Collins, *Regulating Contracts*, at 137.

contracting parties, but since the plaintiff company had gone into liquidation the litigation had proceeded on a very different basis. He remarked:

> I am conscious of the fact that the liquidator of the plaintiffs is adopting an attitude which, had the company not been in liquidation, would never have been adopted by the directors of the company. The point taken by the liquidator is a technical one, and to some extent unmeritorious. But persons in that position have duties to perform, and it is sometimes necessary for them to take points which others would be reluctant to take; and they are entitled, like all others, to have each point considered and decided in accordance with the established principles of law.[109]

Scholars differ over what is the prime motivating factor in the decision whether parties choose legal or non-legal sanctions and norms to govern their relationship. Bernstein would seem to believe it depends on the stage of the contracting relationship. For Charny the decision the parties make over which system will be paramount depends upon the interplay of drafting and enforcement costs.[110] He has pointed out that some relationships are simply better suited to legal enforcement:

> One type is the commitment that is easily specified – so that litigation is straightforward, with predictable outcomes – and for which there are high stakes relative to litigation costs. A second type is the high stakes commitment that will be subsequently interpreted only with much information, particularly with regard to damages. In contrast, vaguer commitments whose interpretation depends on 'embedded' norms or expert decisionmaking, and commitments that have low stakes relative to litigation costs, appear better suited for nonlegal sanctions.[111]

For Kraus and Walt the dual regime for contractual regulation, where the informal contractual performance is at odds with the formal contractual requirements, might be motivated by parties' views about their contracting partners. The former might be optimal

109 [1982] QB 84, 101.
110 Charny, 'Non-legal Sanctions'.
111 Ibid., Charny, 408–9.

among good faith contractors, where trust is more evident, the latter among bad faith (or what are suspected of being bad faith) contractors.[112] The answer to when parties will depend on one or the other system of enforcement probably lies in a combination of all these factors. However, what is relevant for our purposes is that there appears to be almost universal scepticism that the courts can be the arbiters of the relational aspects of the parties' agreement, although some argue that the courts can adapt and become a more suitable forum.[113] The point here is that for contracting parties that contemplate litigation as the manner of solving their disputes, the attempt to reduce their obligations to writing and limit the court's consideration *to* that writing has manifest plausibility as reflecting a genuine intent.

The existence of contextual materials

Another difficulty for the contextual approach is in relation to the existence and use of material that might be important to context or factual matrix: trade customs.[114] Bernstein has again done some important, and controversial, work in relation to the existence of trade customs. Bernstein's work is in the context of the Uniform Commercial Code, which maintains at Article 2–202 (although this incorporationist spirit is repeated elsewhere) that, unless the intention is found to be otherwise, the written agreement can be supplemented 'by course of performance, course of dealing, or usage of trade'. In one article she examines a range of merchant industries and their national associations' attempts at the turn of the last century to codify customs of the trade into rules.[115] She discovered that only very localised, not industrywide, trade customs existed. She concludes that while trade customs do not consistently exist, nevertheless 'merchants do consider it valuable to have an understanding of the ways transactions are usually done, an understanding gleaned from a rough aggregation of practices in the market as a whole.'[116] This knowledge is useful in the early stages of a contracting relationship, when the parties are trying to assess who will perform and who

---

112 Op. cit., 211–12.
113 Collins, *Regulating Contracts*, pp 9–10, and chs 4 and 8.
114 See, general discussion, in op. cit., Gava and Greene, 621–6.
115 Bernstein, 'Questionable Basis'.
116 Ibid., Bernstein, at 716–17.

will default, but becomes less important as the relationship develops. This claim about custom is highly controversial, however, critics arguing that the findings raise 'questions of evidence rather than challenge the entire approach of the UCC'[117] or that 'research into discrete industries, while valuable, is very inconclusive on the desires of business people more generally'[118] or that the time in which the availability of customs is examined (turn of the last century) tells us nothing about the existence of customs here and now.[119] However, her argument is not that trade customs do not exist, but that uniform industrywide trade customs do not exist, and as such she casts doubt on whether custom can provide any sort of consistent normative framework for deciding disputes across particular industries. For some, that customs might only exist on a local level is enough to justify their incorporation in local disputes.[120] This might cause a problem for courts, though, since if local customs are used to resolve a dispute this reduces the case's general precedential value across the industry (which again has implications for costs). Alternatively, in another dispute the local custom may mistakenly be given 'industrywide' relevance by a court. The existence of a custom that is over and above 'the way in which that particular [contractor] has become habituated to doing business' is notoriously difficult to prove.[121] An alternative criticism of the custom dispute is that the identification of applicable customs is, in part, an act of interpretation where the 'normative premises' of the judge must play a role.[122] The judge must distinguish and define the precise scope of the custom. This turns the application of customs into a species of 'moral reflection'. The problem here is that there are also other competing sorts of 'moral reflection' such as economic analysis or philosophy.[123] Given the doubts and ambiguity about custom, it is plausible that parties might

---

117 Macaulay, 'Relational Contracts Floating on a Sea of Custom?', 787–8. See, also, Macaulay 'Real Deal', 65–8.
118 Op. cit., Woodward, 980–1.
119 Op. cit., Kraus and Walt, 202.
120 Ibid., Kraus and Walt.
121 Lord Devlin, 'The Relationship between Commercial Law and Commercial Practice', 251.
122 Craswell, R., 'Do Trade Customs Exist?' in Kraus and Walt (eds), *The Jurisprudential Foundations of Corporate and Commercial Law*, 118.
123 Ibid., Craswell, 142.

wish to ensure that trade custom is ousted altogether in solving interpretative disputes.[124]

Conclusion

This chapter has attempted to demonstrate that there are cogent arguments for courts to adopt a more formalist interpretation strategy in some commercial contracting circumstances. Formalism may manifest itself in a desire for the documents to be taken as the primary evidence of what was agreed, without recourse to negotiations, trade customs, previous understandings or any other extrinsic material. It may also be manifest in a requirement that the terms within the documents be interpreted according to plain meaning. Of course, many contractors will be satisfied that contextualism represents the current interpretative default. But it cannot be ruled out that some commercial contractors will have a preference for a more formal interpretative method to be applied to their agreement, for the reasons already examined. The scope is there then, for parties to attempt to control this aspect of the agreement themselves. This does not seek to deny the importance of contextualism, but instead seeks to place formalism within a broadly contextual approach. If the question whether some parties would prefer a more formalistic approach to contractual interpretation can only be answered by empirical studies, then nothing can be gained by trying to promote the relative merits of formalism on the basis of abstract theoretical enquiries. What is clear is that any impetus towards formalism must come from the parties themselves. This chapter has tried to give some indications of the broad reasons why some parties might choose formalism. The final chapter considers some means by which parties can communicate this choice to the courts.

---

124 For example, *Exxonmobil Sales And Supply Corporation v Texaco Ltd (The Helene Knutsen)* [2003] EWHC 1964 (Comm).

Chapter 5

Controlling interpretation

It is important for contracting parties to identify the current interpretative default that English courts adopt, and to assess whether they would prefer to opt out of it by stipulating the interpretative method they would wish to be applied to their agreement. While the current default would seem to be contextual interpretation, the interpretation of the text remains the paramount concern. Courts will refer to the factual background of the contract, commercial purposes and so on, in an attempt to come to an understanding of the parties' agreement, rather than engage in a detailed linguistic analysis of the words in the document. Although contextual interpretation is the current default, presently, the courts' contextual enquiries are fairly limited. But it was noted in Chapter 3 that developments in the law on prior negotiations suggest that some expansion of the admissible context is imminent, if not already occurring. If this expanded contextualism becomes the relevant interpretative default, then parties that want a contextual or flexible approach to their agreement need do nothing. Provided the parties have some degree of trust in the courts to reach the decision that they would have agreed between themselves, they might leave much of their contract open-ended, with context (including negotiations, etc.) filling in the gaps. However, parties that would prefer a judge not to rely on 'commercial instinct', or extrinsic material may need to take steps to communicate this to the courts, rather than rely on the elusive 'context' to do this for them. In the choice between form or substance in contractual interpretation, an important influencing factor must be what the contracting parties would choose.[1] Parties will of

---

1   Katz, A.W., 'The Economics of Form and Substance in Contract Interpretation' (2004) 104 *Col LR* 496, 514.

course differ over how they perceive, and make, the trade-offs between form and substance.[2] But it ought to be open to the parties to impose a parol evidence rule on their agreement, since they can no longer be sure that the rule represents the current interpretative default. This chapter assesses some of the methods the parties may employ to do this.

Choosing interpretative method

The parties' preference for formalism, where it exists, cannot always take precedence. Interpretation cannot be completely divorced from context and much will depend upon the nature of the interpretative dispute before the courts. But there are certainly some interpretative disputes where the parties' stipulation as to how they wished their agreement to be interpreted would be a material factor to consider. Such a possibility must be inherent in any contextual approach to interpretation. Some might argue that English contract law, particularly its commercial law, is already sensitive to the kinds of consideration that appeared in the last chapter, and will use a more formal interpretative method when this appears to support the 'commercial purpose' of the agreement. While courts may be instinctively sensitive to whether the parties would prefer a more or less formal approach, this is not a policy that they are pursuing openly or self-consciously. In *Total v Arco*, Lord Steyn remarked, 'In this legal context an interpretation which gives no effect to the words "condition precedent", so far as it applies to the allocation agreement, ought to be received with an initial sense of incredulity.'[3] What are omitted here are the reasons why, *in that case*, the legal context is taken to be the governing one. Why should the documents regulate the agreement, over and above the fact that the documents are simply available? What indications were there that the formal approach to 'condition precedent' was the correct one to take? Investigation of these sorts of factors would save the kind of judicial unease expressed by Lord Hope that the formal approach that was adopted was out of line with the expectations of the parties. The courts rarely ask the question of what kind of interpretative approach the parties wanted, but it is arguable that at least some of the judge's

---

2   Ibid., Katz, 511–12.
3   [1998] 2 Lloyd's Law Rep 209, 222.

justificatory efforts would be better spent pursuing this line of inquiry.[4]

The question of how much control the parties should have over the interpretative method of a court is fraught with difficulty. Judicial statements suggest that the parties' intentions and expectations provide a central justification for interpretative outcomes. But this is countered by the assertion that the interpretation of the contract is a job for the courts, not the parties. As a practical matter, the parties generally interpret contracts since most contracts do not result in litigation.[5] Alternatively, it might be argued that parties can have little control over interpretative method, since many disputes may arise where the contractual wording is genuinely ambiguous or vague, and where it cannot be said that the parties had any intentions or expectations. The very nature of interpretation, coupled with problems related to the indeterminacy of language, makes contextual interpretation a necessity. While this cannot be denied, there is a very wide range of material that can rightly form part of the context. If some parties have gone to the time and expense of drafting a relatively complete document, they may also seek, within its terms, to offer some direction to the court over their 'choice of the interpretative theory that will be used to enforce those terms.'[6]

One obvious difficulty lies in knowing what contracting parties want from their contract law and from the courts. The present assumption of the courts is that commercial parties want 'commercial construction', without anyone being any the wiser about what 'commercial construction' entails, except that it is the antithesis of literalism, which is almost always assumed to give rise to uncommercial results.[7] What contracting parties require is a matter to be determined largely by empirical evidence. Some recent, albeit limited, evidence has been provided by a survey commissioned by law firm Clifford Chance.[8] The survey was conducted in response to

---

4   Bowers, J.W., 'Murphy's Law and The Elementary Theory of Contract Interpretation: A Response to Schwartz and Scott' (2005) 57 *Rutgers L R* 587, 620–1.

5   Smith, *Contract Theory*, 276.

6   Schwartz and Scott, 'Contract Theory and the Limits of Contract Law', 618.

7   See, for example, the criticisms of the Court of Appeal by Lord Steyn in *Sirius v FAI* [2004] UKHL 54, at [25].

8   Vogenauer, S. and Weatherill, S., 'The European Community's Competence to Pursue the Harmonisation of Contract Law – an Empirical Contribution to the Debate' in S. Vogenauer and S. Weatherill (eds) *The Harmonisation of European Contract Law*, 2006, Oxford: Hart Publishing, 105.

European Commission proposals for increased harmonisation of contract law in Member States. The chief aim was to discover if European businesses did find national differences in contract law rules a barrier to trade. The survey sought the views of 175 firms in eight Member States of the European Union. The survey has identified that European businesses 'want their contract law, in decreasing order of importance, to enable trade and to be fair, predictable, short and concise, flexible and prescriptive'.[9] Here, there are a range of considerations in operation, not all of which pull in the same direction. The qualities of flexibility, fairness and predictability, for example, may often conflict. These are difficult considerations to balance, but there is no convincing argument as to why the courts should be better able to carry out this balancing than the parties. The trade-offs that can be made between form and substance depend on criteria that are better assessed by the parties themselves.[10] Judges often show sensitivity to the question of whether, and how, commercial contract law reflects what commercial parties want. As Lord Devlin wrote, 'The knowledge that if a customer does not like your wares he may go elsewhere – to arbitration, or to the courts of another country – is salutary'.[11]

Methods of control

The next task is to consider how the parties might exercise greater interpretative control over their agreement, or how they might be able to reduce the scope of context to influence the meaning placed on their agreement. The kind of contextual material of interest here is that which may have the effect of altering, or adding to, the agreed statement of terms. This might be material from previous contracts, oral conversations prior, or subsequent, to the contract, previous negotiations, trade customs, or understandings generated by the

9 Ibid., 136. In relation to the choice of a regime of contract law to govern their dealings, the following were the most important considerations: 'enable trade' – 87 per cent; 'predictable' – 79 per cent; 'fair' – 78 per cent; 'flexible' – 66 per cent; 'short and concise' – 61 per cent; 'prescriptive' – 39 per cent; 'other' – 12 per cent. Ibid., 121–2, note 51.
10 Katz, 'The Relative Costs of Incorporating Trade Usage', 184. For the considerations in making the trade-off between form and substance, see Katz, 'Form and Substance', 535–7.
11 Devlin, 'The Relationship Between Commercial Law and Commercial Practice', 250.

market in which the parties conduct business. The consideration here is how far the parties might reduce, even if they cannot entirely eliminate, the possibility that considerations of context alter their obligations. Of course, one can say that contracting parties do choose interpretative methods by using courts and litigation as the manner of solving the dispute. As Barnett notes, 'by invoking the system of legal enforcement, one is implicitly accepting that the legal system may be called upon to interpret the agreement and fill any gaps.'[12] But consideration of more direct ways the parties can influence interpretation methods is rare. In particular, the possibility of 'contracting out' of the contextual approach is usually relegated to a footnote in articles supportive of the general shift in interpretative emphasis.[13] McKendrick also recognises that while the discussion of contract doctrine takes up the most space in contract textbooks, cases usually turn on the interpretation of the contract terms incorporated into the agreement by the parties, and this aspect is given very little attention in the books. Discussion of the provisions of self-regulation contained in the parties' agreement loses out to the practically much less important discussion of doctrine.[14]

Katz suggests three possible ways that contracting parties can influence interpretative method: merger (or entire agreement) clauses, choice of law clauses and choice of forum clauses.[15] Choice of law clauses may enable parties to choose a regime characterised by more or less formality, depending on their own particular preferences. English lawyers are perhaps more familiar with overseas parties choosing English law as the regime applicable to their disputes, particularly in the areas of shipping, international trade and finance. It has already been noted that English contract law has the reputation for greater formality than some other regimes. In relation to choice of forum, parties may choose arbitration or mediation over courts if they believe that either forum will be more, or less, formal and less expensive. Commercial parties often prefer to have their disputes settled by arbitration and include clauses in their contracts directing that disputes should be resolved by this method in preference to litigation (although the effect of such clauses is often itself the

---

12 'The Sound of Silence', p 865.
13 See, for example, McMeel, 'Prior Negotiations and Subsequent Conduct', note 97; Macaulay, 'The Real Deal and the Paper Deal', note 25.
14 McKendrick, *The Creation of a European Law of Contracts*, 7–8, 10.
15 Ibid., 507–8.

subject of litigation). Arbitration offers several advantages over courts in dispute resolution. Arbitrators have greater freedom to take into account a wider range of materials and reach a result more tailored to the parties' circumstances, without the fetters that the common law may impose. Parties are usually able to choose their arbitrators, and can thus choose experts in the field of the dispute. The parties are also able to decide how the arbitration proceedings will be conducted and where the arbitration will be held. The arbitrator usually has the power, unless the parties dictate otherwise, to make any enquiries that they see fit, see any documents and decide on the strictness of rules of evidence to be applied.[16] By these mechanisms the parties can exercise a measure of control over the proceedings and can determine both what is interpreted and who interprets it.

Although choice of forum and law are important ways in which the parties can exercise control over interpretative method, this chapter will concentrate on entire agreement clauses[17] as a mechanism for directing courts towards a particular interpretative strategy. This is because the prime concern here is how parties might control interpretative method during the litigation process, and within the contract terms, rather than through alternative dispute resolution mechanisms. While the scope of these clauses varies depending on how they are drafted, in general they stipulate that the obligations and terms of the contract are to be found only in the written form of the agreement and nowhere else. Such a clause may prevent a claimant building a case on the basis of a collateral contract, or an oral promise, representation or assurance made prior to the contract, or even on the basis of some types of implied term. Of course it might be possible for the parties to be more direct in relation to their agreement, by stipulating an 'interpretation clause', which gives a direction to the court as to the interpretation strategy that should be adopted. Entire agreement clauses might be thought to be too indirect a method of influencing interpretation. But the advantage of examining entire agreement clauses is that they are familiar, and their effect has been considered by the courts already (at least the

---

16 See, for example, the Rules of the London Court of International Arbitration, 1998, articles 7.1, 14.1, 16.1 and 22. These are available at http://www.lcia.org/ARB_folder/arb_english_main.htm (accessed 15 September 2006). See, also, Collins, *Regulating Contracts*, 182–7.

17 Commonly called merger, or integration, clauses outside the UK.

lower courts), although there is not a comprehensive body of law relating to them. The law's attitude towards entire agreement clauses may at least give an indication of how a court might react to a more tailored 'interpretation clause'.

Entire agreement clauses (EACs)

An EAC is usually phrased along the following lines: 'This contract comprises the entire agreement between the parties, as detailed in the various Articles and Annexures and there are not any agreements, understandings, promises or conditions, oral or written, expressed or implied, concerning the subject matter which are not merged into this contract and superseded hereby.'[18] In *Alman v Associated News*,[19] the term was to the effect that the written contract constituted 'the entire agreement and understanding between the parties with respect to all matters therein referred to'. The judge accepted that such a term could exclude any collateral contracts and warranties arising out of the parties' bilateral understandings,[20] but not, as a matter of construction, a claim for misrepresentation. If the issue is whether the governing framework of the agreement is the written contract or 'reasonable expectations' (assuming these to arise 'extra-contractually'),[21] then the entire agreement clause appears to give a definitive answer in favour of the written contract. An initial difficulty is that many will be sceptical about whether these clauses, like other so-called boilerplate terms, can be taken seriously as an expression of the intentions of the parties. As has been noted, the core of the contextualist critique is that the written documents are perhaps the least important element of the parties' agreement. Therefore, any statement in the documents that they represent the complete agreement must carry little weight. Such statements are a product of the parties' lawyers, rather than the parties themselves.[22] The question of

---

18 *Deepak Fertilisers v ICI Chemicals Ltd* [1999] 1 Lloyds Rep 387. Acknowledgements of non-reliance and nullifications of previous contracts have a slightly different effect and are not considered here.
19 *Alman v Associated News* ChD, unreported, 20 June 1980.
20 Cf. the earlier decision of *Brikom Investments Ltd v Carr* [1979] 2 All ER 753.
21 Collins, H., 'The Research Agenda of Implicit Dimensions of Contracts', in D. Campbell, H. Collins and J. Wightman (eds), *Implicit Dimensions of Contract*, 2003, Oxford: Hart Publishing, 3. See, also, Posner, E., 'The Parol Evidence Rule', 534.
22 Collins, *Regulating Contracts*, p 159.

whether these clauses are included after deliberation and reflection, or without any thought at all, cannot be answered in the abstract. Whether commercial parties understand the implications of these clauses, and if so, the reasons why they might include them are issues that can be resolved only by reference to the parties themselves.[23] Given that commercial contracting parties are not a homogeneous group, the answers will vary.

Such clauses also raise problems about fairness, but it is not intended to deal with those here. While it is no doubt correct that some categories of commercial contractor need protection from some varieties of term,[24] the issues raised are arguably not very different to those that have already been well rehearsed in relation to exclusions and limitations of liability. It will suffice to say here that, if we frame the issue in terms of whether such clauses offend against fairness, then the arguments run both ways. Certainly use of such clauses can be a mandate to lie and mislead in negotiation without fear of contractual consequences.[25] It is no doubt true that 'the worst reason to seek more formality in interpretation is to obtain legal sanction for what amounts to a form of deception'.[26] But it can also be unfair to go 'threshing through the undergrowth and finding in the course of negotiations some (chance) remark or statement (often long forgotten or difficult to recall or explain) on which to found a claim . . . to the existence of a collateral warranty'.[27]

What justification is there for thinking that EACs can have any influence on interpretation? There are cases that demonstrate the effectiveness of an EAC in limiting the range of contextual material available for consideration by the judge. In limiting the admissible context, or 'background', themselves, the parties may reduce the options for a judge seeking to give effect to implicit understandings or reasonable expectations at the expense of contract terms. For example, an EAC may disable a court from giving effect to understandings generated by context through techniques of collateral contracts and implication. Some support for this view of EACs

---

23 Woodward, 'Neoformalism', 984.
24 The Law Commission identify EACs as an example of 'potentially unfair clauses against which businesses, unlike consumers, are not currently protected', Law Com Report No 292 *Unfair Terms in Contracts* (2005) at para 2.31.
25 Macaulay, 'Real Deal', 62.
26 Woodward, 'Neoformalism', 991.
27 Per Lightman J., *The Inntrepreneur Pub Co v East Crown Ltd* (Ch D) [2000] 3 E.G.L.R. 31 at [7].

was demonstrated in the case of *Inntrepreneur Pub Company v East Crown Ltd.*[28] *East Crown* was a test case concerning whether tenants of public houses were bound by an exclusive purchasing obligation ('beer tie') in their leases with Inntrepreneur. The historical context of the case was particularly important. The tied public house was a feature of the British brewing and pub trade for many years. Breweries owned pubs, which they let to tenants, and imposed a beer tie that required the tenants to purchase beer from the brewery. In 1989 a report by the Monopolies and Mergers Commission (now Competition Commission) recommended scaling back the number of tied public houses. As a result of the Supply of Beer (Tied Estates) Order 1989, many breweries were required to dispose of substantial parts of their tied estates.[29] Instead of simply selling off estates, breweries formed nominally separate companies ('pubcos'), which took over their public house ownership.[30] Since pubcos were largely formed and controlled by breweries, they continued to impose beer ties on tenants. Inntrepreneur was such a pubco formed between breweries Grand Metropolitan plc and Courage Ltd. Inntrepreneur's tied pubs were required to purchase their beer and drinks from Courage or other nominated suppliers. Given the degree of vertical integration between beer brewing and retailing here, before the formation of Inntrepreneur could go ahead, Courage and Grand Met were required to give undertakings to the Secretary of State for Trade and Industry that any pubs remaining in Inntrepreneur's ownership on 28 March 1998 would be released from the beer tie by that date. The undertakings did not apply to any tied house sold by Inntrepreneur before 28 March 1998. On formation in March 1991, Inntrepreneur owned about 8,450 pubs. Over the next few years, they sold some pubs and released others from the tie so that by the middle of 1995 their number of tied houses had fallen to less than 3,000. By this time, Inntrepreneur had also severed most of its connections with the UK brewing industry. It applied for a release from the undertakings in June 1996 and this was granted in February 1997.

---

28 One of many cases brought against Inntrepreneur and Courage Ltd by disaffected pub tenants. See, also, *Inntrepreneur Pub Company v Sweeney* [2002] EWHC 1060 (Ch D); cf. *1406 Pub Company Ltd v Hoare* (Ch D, unreported, 2 March 2001).
29 S.I. 1989/2390 (one of the so-called 'Beer Orders').
30 Second Report from the Trade and Industry Committee, Session 2004–05, *Pub Companies*, HC 128-I, 21 December 2004.

The pubs that remained in Inntrepreneur's hands at this time were therefore still subject to the beer tie.

It is within this context that on 3 October 1996, Inntrepreneur leased a pub to the defendant for a term of 30 years after the defendant's previous lease expired. There had been some four years of negotiations leading up to the grant of the new lease. The defendant's representative, Mr Hickey, had signed a 'lease acceptance form' in May 1996 and an 'agreement for lease' three months later. This agreement contained a clause stating that it constituted the entire agreement between the parties. It also contained a beer tie. The defendant's pub was not one of the ones sold off by Inntrepreneur, nor released from the tie, but by April 1998 the defendant was no longer purchasing any beer from the nominated supplier. Inntrepreneur sought an injunction to prevent the defendant buying beer outside the tie and damages for breach of contract. The defendant claimed Inntrepreneur, through its representatives, had given a collateral warranty to Mr Hickey that he was released from the tie with effect from 28 March 1998. Mr Hickey was aware that Inntrepreneur had applied for a release from its undertakings, but he nevertheless maintained that in the previous four years of negotiations with representatives of Inntrepreneur, the claimant had contractually promised that he would be released from the tie.

The judge held that the EAC in the agreement for lease was sufficient to bind the parties to the terms of the agreement, including the tie. He said:

> such a clause constitutes a binding agreement between the parties that the full contractual terms are to be found in the document containing the clause and not elsewhere, and that accordingly any promises or assurances made in the course of the negotiations (which in the absence of such a clause might have effect as a collateral warranty) shall have no contractual force, save insofar as they are reflected and given effect in that document.[31]

The clause provided 'in law a complete answer to any claim by [East] Crown based on the alleged collateral warranty'.[32] The significant effect of this for our purposes was that the judge said he was not

31 [2000] 3 EGLR 31, at [7].
32 Ibid., at [8].

required to determine if the collateral warranty was ever given. Although he did go on to consider this, some significant contextual material would have been excluded from consideration had the judge held to this line. There had been some four years of prior negotiations, with four different Inntrepreneur representatives, all seeking to persuade Mr Hickey to take out the new lease. Clearly, Mr Hickey's beliefs were not just subjective. Inntrepreneur also intended that the tenants would be released from the tie since their promotional literature distributed to tenants stated as much.[33] But this was marked 'subject to contract'. One of Inntrepreneur's representatives admitted that in seeking to persuade Mr Hickey to take out the lease they had talked of the effect of the undertakings and the release from the tie. But the judge thought that the defendant's belief about the release was induced by the existence of the undertakings (to which he was not a party) and, in his opinion, none of Inntrepreneur's actions constituted a promise to release the defendant from the tie, notwithstanding that seeking the revocation of the undertakings was under the claimant's complete control. The judge noted that Mr Hickey was an 'intelligent and able negotiator and astute businessman with no particular knowledge of the law and no more than a layman's understanding of the effect of the Undertakings',[34] but that he had also received legal advice. Evidently the court did not believe itself to be in the best position to regulate competition in the beer distribution and pub trade and no doubt this is correct. Nevertheless, *Inntrepreneur v East Crown* demonstrates the potential of the EAC to reduce the scope of context as a source of additional obligations that might better reflect the real understandings of the parties, based on the social context of the agreement.

There is also authority that suggests that EACs might prevent a court implying certain kinds of term into an agreement in order to give effect to contextual understandings. An illustration is provided by *Exxonmobil Sales And Supply Corporation v Texaco Ltd* (*The Helene Knutsen*).[35] This was an application for summary judgment in a dispute concerning a sale of diesel from the claimants (Exxon) to the defendants (Texaco). Texaco claimed to be entitled to reject the diesel on the basis that it did not comply with the contract specification according to the testing procedures carried out at the port of

---

33 Ibid., at [13].
34 Ibid., at [17].
35 [2003] EWHC 1964 (Comm).

discharge. The contract was arguably ambiguous over the testing procedure that was to be applied: one procedure was supported by the wording of the contract and a slightly different procedure by trade usage. The cargo was on specification under the former procedure, but the latter procedure had not been followed. The contract stated that it contained 'the entire agreement of the parties with respect to the subject matter hereof and there is no other promise, representation, warranty, usage or course of dealing affecting it'. After Texaco rejected the cargo, Exxon sold it elsewhere and sought damages for repudiatory breach. Texaco argued that the inspection procedure supported by trade usage or custom was to be implied into the contract. While Texaco's real motives in rejecting the cargo might be questioned, the material consideration here is the effect of the EAC on the attempt to imply a term based on trade usage. The judge accepted that a custom regarding testing procedure could be established, but denied it could be implied into the contract because of the effect of the EAC.[36] The judge said, 'the agreement that "there is no usage" is a clear indication that the parties intended that terms based upon usage or custom were not to be implied into the sale agreement.'[37] The judge distinguished a term implied on the basis of 'business efficacy', however. Such a term is required to make the contract work and is part of the entire contract *ab initio*.[38] Here, one can see how the EAC precludes the generation of a protracted interpretative dispute by preventing one party asserting (or manufacturing) ambiguity in the terms of the contract by reference to a custom. Context was not permitted to override express terms.

Can EACs influence interpretation?

Inntrepreneur and *Exxonmobil* give an indication of the potential of the EAC to render ineffective some judicial techniques for incorporating understandings generated by context into an agreement. Sceptics may argue that EACs are simply an attempt to resurrect the parol evidence rule, and should not be taken seriously. Or it may be

36 Ibid., at [24] citing *Inntrepreneur v East Crown*.
37 Ibid.
38 Ibid., at [27]. See, also, *SERE v Volkswagen* [2004] EWHC 1551 at [28] and *Hotel Services Ltd v Hilton International Hotels Ltd* (CA, unreported 5 February 1999), where it was doubted that an EAC could prevent implication of terms on the necessity test.

argued that while an EAC can prevent additional obligations arising that were not anticipated by the original agreement, it can have no effect on how the written terms are to be interpreted. These arguments are considered below.

Resurrecting the parol evidence rule

McMeel suggests that EACs 'do not restrict the courts to the four corners of the contract in determining what obligations the parties have undertaken. The contrary view would resuscitate the now discredited parol evidence rule'.[39] The Law Commission also maintained that without legislation an EAC could not have conclusive effect.[40] Collins too comes close to saying such clauses should simply be ignored.[41] But to accept EACs as potentially effective is not the same as applying a strict parol evidence rule. The parol evidence rule was based on an inference from the *appearance* of the documents, whereas an EAC is ostensibly a clearer indication of the parties' intentions. The parol evidence rule may be discredited as a rule of common law, but it is surely a different matter if the parties themselves write the rule into the contract. The reasons why the parties may choose to include an EAC are not identical to why the courts might prefer to apply a parol evidence rule, although there is a good deal of overlap in the arguments. So, for example, the parol evidence rule might be attractive to the courts because of its administrative convenience,[42] although this would not appear to be a compelling reason for the parties to include an EAC in their contracts, unless such convenience is expressed in terms of the time and cost of litigation. An EAC can also extend much further than the parol evidence rule, particularly when one considers the truncated version of the rule cited by Lord

---

39 'Prior Negotiations And Subsequent Conduct', note 97. McMeel doubts that the parol evidence rule still exists: ibid., note 32.
40 Op. cit., Law Commission No 154, para 2.15.
41 Collins, *Regulating Contracts*, 159–60. In a later article with D. Campbell, his position is more circumspect, acknowledging that not all contractual planning documents are the same: 'Discovering the Implicit Dimensions of Contract' in *Implicit Dimensions*, 25 at 42. Although at 41 they also write, 'such deliberate statements [entire agreement clauses] indicate a special state of mind, which is unlikely to be present in most transactions'.
42 Greenfield, M., 'Consumer Protection And The Uniform Commercial Code: The Role Of Assent In Article 2 And Article 9' (1997) 75 *Washington U L Q* 289, 309; Smith, S., *Contract Theory*, 275.

Hoffmann in his *Investors* restatement. In Lord Hoffmann's judgment, the application of the parol evidence rule is limited to the admission of previous negotiations and declarations of subjective intent.[43] The case of *Exxonmobil v Texaco* illustrates the wider potential of the EAC beyond the operation of the parol evidence rule. Given the potential that contextualism offers for increasing the information available to the court in undertaking contractual interpretation, it can hardly be surprising that some contracting parties might attempt to restrict the available information through contract terms.

Identifying and interpreting obligations

A more serious objection is that EACs are a wholly inappropriate method of cutting off judicial recourse to context and the implicit understandings of the parties. This is because the real function of such clauses is to prevent new causes of action emerging that were not contemplated or included in the written agreement. Thus they can have no effect on the decision as to what the terms in the written agreement mean. Evidence of negotiations, for example, would only be used to interpret unclear elements in the final documents, not to give rise to any new obligations. Implicit understandings and context may also have a role in determining *not only what the usual written contract says, but when it can be taken to mean what it says*.[44] Thus context may still be important in determining whether the EAC is a genuine expression of the parties' intentions.

The thrust of the argument here is that EACs can only have a fairly benign evidential function. The EAC can only tell us where, according to the parties, a complete statement of their obligations can be found. Whatever documents are identified as 'contractual', these documents cannot be self-interpreting, and so nothing in an EAC can prevent a court adopting a contextual approach to interpretation of the terms. In short, EACs are only concerned with identification and not meaning. Thus while the clause may disable a court from using certain doctrines to supplement the contract with additional obligations, it cannot oust the process of 'contextual interpretation'

---

43 [1998] 1 All ER 98, 114–15.
44 Wightman, J., 'Beyond Custom: Contract, Contexts, and the Recognition of Implicit Understandings' in *Implicit Dimensions*, 158 (emphasis in the original). See, also, op. cit., Campbell and Collins, p 42.

to the extent that this is perceived as a different process to other 'amending' techniques.

The success of this argument depends upon a distinction being drawn between interpretation and 'other tasks', including the identification of a provision as a 'contractual obligation'. It has already been argued that it is difficult to see such a clear distinction at work in contract law. Nevertheless, many contract instruments uphold a difference between identifying contractual obligations and their interpretation. For example, the UNIDROIT principles draw this distinction in article 2.17:

> a contract in writing which contains a clause indicating that the writing completely embodies the terms on which the parties have agreed cannot be contradicted or supplemented by evidence of prior statements or agreements. However, such statements or agreements may be used to interpret the writing.[45]

Thus the use of an entire agreement clause can prevent extraneous material from being identified as giving rise to additional contractual obligations, but it cannot prevent such material being used in the interpretation of the agreement. This casts doubt on whether the identification of what constitutes 'the contractual documents' can be regarded as an instance of interpretation.

This understanding of the operation of EACs as concerned with identification and limitation of obligations, but not their interpretation, is reinforced by the recent judgment of the Court of Appeal in *ProForce Recruit Ltd v Rugby Group Ltd.*[46] Although not involving a trial of the substantive issues (the question being whether the claimant could establish that they had a real prospect of success at trial), the case directly addresses the nature of the relationship between an entire agreement clause and contextual interpretation. The facts have already been stated.[47] One of the most important questions was whether negotiations prior to contract would be admissible evidence in the interpretation of the phrase 'preferred supplier status' in the parties' agreement. Clause 9.2 of that agreement stipulated that 'This Agreement together with any other document expressed to being operated herein constitutes the entire contract between the parties

---

45 See also 2:105 PECL.
46 [2006] EWCA Civ 69.
47 See Chapter 3.

and supersedes all prior representations, agreements, negotiations or understandings whether oral or in writing.' The defendant argued that this clause precluded the court from considering prior negotiations in deciding the meaning of the term. The obvious difficulty was that there was no definition or explanation of the contentious phrase in the contract, nor did it have a natural meaning. The Court of Appeal was not prepared to concede as a matter of principle that the EAC could prevent the court considering previous negotiations. Mummery LJ drew a distinction between:

> ascertaining the contents of a written contract or setting up a collateral or side contract by reference to prior representations, agreements, negotiations and understandings and, on the other hand, ascertaining the meaning of a term contained in a written contract by reference to pre-contract materials. It is reasonably arguable that in clause 9.2 the parties intended to exclude the former, but not to inhibit the latter.[48]

Arden LJ agreed that the issue was as to the identification of 'the meaning that the parties in effect incorporated into their agreement'. On this basis it seems that the prior negotiations were no longer prior negotiations – the matters decided upon were incorporated into the contract as the meaning of the disputed term. Arden LJ's explanation has two particular advantages. First, giving effect to the meaning attributed to the phrase in negotiations was not giving effect to the subjective intentions of the parties; rather, it was enforcing the contract according to its terms. Second, the agreed meaning was part of the 'entire agreement' and thus could not be affected by the terms of the EAC. Arden LJ compared the situation where the parties have expressly dealt with the meaning to be attributed to terms in the contract. She remarked:

> there is no reason in principle why a contract should not expressly state that a particular term used in the contract should bear the meaning which the parties gave to it in the course of their negotiations. Evidence as to the parties' negotiations would in those circumstances unquestionably be admissible to show what that meaning was.[49]

48 Ibid., at [41].
49 Ibid., at [54].

And later:

> In addition, the evidence may in due course show that the parties
> in effect agreed that their agreement or common understanding
> as to the meaning of 'preferred supplier status' was to displace
> anything in the written agreement that would otherwise override
> that meaning. There is in my judgment, a sufficient prospect of
> success on that ground also.[50]

In these two passages there is tacit acceptance, both that the parties
can affect interpretative method by the express terms of their agreement *and* that evidence can be adduced to override the express terms
of their agreement on the basis of the parties' common understandings. No guidance is given as to which takes precedence when these,
invariably, conflict. With respect, while Arden LJ has appreciated
that the parties can include terms giving guidance on meaning, she
has not conceded that the parties in this case did just that by including an EAC that precisely stipulated that prior negotiations were
superseded by the contract, and were *not* to be treated as part of the
contract. If the parties can effectively contract *in* to the use of prior
negotiations in deciding on contract meaning, as Arden LJ allows,
then it must be open to them to contract *out* of such use. If extrinsic
evidence can show that the parties agreed that their understanding
as to 'preferred supplier status' was to displace anything in the written agreement, such evidence can also go to show that the parties
intended to be bound by all the terms of the written agreement, and
not their common understandings or negotiations. What is required
is some way of arbitrating between the terms and the understandings. Of course, one way is simply to deny effectiveness to the 'boilerplate' provisions in the place of 'individually negotiated' terms.
But the question of whether the EAC was included without reflection,
or was included only after careful thought and planning, is surely as
much a contextual enquiry as to what the phrase 'preferred supplier
status' means.

The reply to this might be twofold. First, it might be argued – why
put a reference to 'preferred supplier status' in the contract at all if
the parties did not have any intentions about how that term should
be interpreted? If prior negotiations shed light on that meaning, then

---

50 Ibid., at [59].

why exclude their use? The answer is that the parties may have meant something or they may have meant nothing by the inclusion of the term 'preferred supplier status', just as they may have meant something or they may have meant nothing by the inclusion of the EAC. The 'preferred supplier status' clause might have been an attempt to write trust and reassurance into the agreement – perhaps as an attempt to show goodwill, or a willingness to co-operate – rather than a binding legal obligation. Thus the term may be irrelevant to the legal framework, but relevant only to the social context, and ProForce are attempting to assert relationship-preserving norms in an endgame situation. If we say that the provision must have been intended as a binding legal obligation, otherwise why include it in the written contract, then we can turn the same argument on the EAC and impart that term with legal significance. Much of the judgment in *ProForce* is given over to the question of whether previous negotiations should be admissible to assist with interpretation, but the parties had arguably dealt with this by including an EAC. If the parties stipulate that all their understandings are incorporated into the contract, and all prior negotiations are superseded, then the effect of this is that it is up to the court to determine the meaning to be attached to 'preferred supplier status' without reference to any contextual material that the parties have excluded. We have seen that there are cogent reasons why the parties might wish to exclude evidence of what was said or done in negotiations from a judge's consideration. The correct contextual question is as to the relative importance of the contract terms and how the parties might have wanted their agreement to be interpreted. Naturally, this forms no part of the deliberations in the appeal court.

The second consideration is that if reference to preliminary negotiations is ruled out of account by the operation of the EAC, then there is no context within which the clause can be interpreted. Since prior negotiations provide the only context in which the term can be understood, they must be admissible. But courts are frequently called upon to determine meanings where it is not clear what was intended, where alternative meanings are possible and when there appears to be no available context, commercial purpose or background to guide them. In *Deutsche Genossenschaftsbank v Burnhope*, Lord Nicholls remarked, 'In the ordinary course one would hope that the commercial purpose intended to be achieved by the words under consideration would cast light on how the words should sensibly be understood. There is no assistance to be gained from that quarter in this case.'[51] In situations where there is judged to be 'no context', the judge may fall back on natural meaning as the relevant default, or else rely on their 'commercial instinct'.[52] A judge in this position would simply have to do the best they could. This is exactly what the trial judge did in *ProForce v Rugby*. He interpreted 'preferred supplier status' without reference to prior negotiations. The possibility that the parties may have preferred the phrase to be interpreted by the judge in a court, and to have the judge's meaning attributed to it, is not considered by the Court of Appeal.

A further argument is that an EAC cannot oust the interpretative function of the court in a case like *ProForce* precisely because it is the *function of the court*, and not the parties, to decide what the contract means. But does this mean the courts can decide which terms to enforce and which to ignore? Of course it seems more appropriate to ignore the boilerplate provision, rather than the individually negotiated and discussed term, but the issue is how the parties wanted their agreement to be understood. The parties' own choice must be an important consideration in determining the correct context for understanding the contractual relationship. Of course, if it is decided that the relationship bore more of the hallmarks of a relational, rather than a discrete, transaction, then the courts are probably correct to consider prior negotiations. But the courts need a framework of considerations to be able to determine this issue. The correct contextual inquiry in a case like *ProForce* relates to the parties' attitude towards the terms of their agreement. What was there in the context to suggest that the parties placed more emphasis on the provision concerning 'preferred supplier status' than the EAC? Were there particular reasons why the parties might have wanted to exclude previous negotiations from consideration – for example because of the unreliability or high turnover of negotiating staff and employees, or because Rugby wanted to maintain flexibility over staff provision, and ProForce were aware of that? Once these contextual matters are considered it will be appreciated that it is difficult to maintain a clear distinction between identifying obligations and interpreting them. Here an additional obligation (to offer contracts to ProForce first) is in danger of being implied into the agreement when it is by no means clear that this is what the parties intended. The courts should be very

---

51 [1995] 1 WLR 1580.
52 Mance LJ in *Sinochem v Mobil* said the only background was the court's 'instinctive appreciation of commercial likelihood', at [24].

slow in imposing such additional obligations on the parties in this manner, particularly when the terms of the contract expressly direct the court not to consider evidence of prior negotiations.

Evading the EAC

None of this means that the EAC should have conclusive, or even presumptive, effect. As with all interpretation matters, that must depend upon the context. There are a range of techniques open to a court to impugn an entire agreement clause if they are not satisfied that its inclusion is genuine. In such circumstances, the courts can look behind the written documents. Some instances of this occur in circumstances when the parol evidence rule would also be treated as having no application. For example, if the written documents are not regarded as complete, or when the written document is silent as to a particular material factor, it may be supplemented by other evidence.[53] A judge could adopt a flexible interpretation of what constitutes the contractual documents.[54] The doctrines of waiver,[55] promissory estoppel,[56] rectification[57] or post-contractual variation[58] could be pressed into service. Or EACs could be subject to the legislation designed to curb unfair terms without doing too much violence to the statutory scheme.[59] One example of these mechanisms will suffice here. In *Fulton v Toyota*[60] an agreement specified that the contract could be terminated on giving two years notice. The form also contained an EAC along the following lines:

> The provisions of this Agreement and the documents herein referred to shall constitute the entire agreement between the parties, and no collateral warranty whether written or oral shall have

---

53 For example *Cyprotex Discovery Ltd v University of Sheffield* [2004] EWCA Civ 380, at [63]. A conversation prior to contract was held to be part of the contract, despite the presence of an EAC, since the written terms and the oral conversation did not relate to the same thing.

54 *Fulton v Toyota*, unreported, 23 July 1999.

55 *SAM v Hedley* [2002] EWHC 2733.

56 *Brikom Investments v Carr* [1979] 2 All ER 753.

57 *Hurst Stores & Interiors Ltd v ML Europe Property Ltd* [2004] EWCA Civ 490.

58 *Hotel Aida Opera SARL v Golden Tulip Worldwide BV* [2004] EWHC 1012, at [91].

59 Such clauses perhaps falling foul of s 3(2)(b)(i) UCTA 1977. See *SAM v Hedley* [2002] EWHC 2733, at [62].

60 CA Unreported, 23 July 1999.

any legal effect and . . . no variation of the terms hereof shall have legal effect unless in writing and signed by both parties.

The court held that this comprehensive term was nevertheless ineffective to oust evidence of a letter submitted with the agreement that stated the true understandings of all the parties, which the contract between them was to terminate after one year. The letter was interpreted as a contractual document.[61] The judge made the observation that 'in the present case the parties could not have intended the form of agreement including the entire agreement clause to express the entire agreement between them'. Of course, it is only by reference to context that this seemingly contradictory statement makes any sort of sense: the implicit understandings fix the obligations, even if this contradicts the express terms of the written document. It was clear that both claimants and defendants were aware that the correct understanding was expressed in the letter and not the written 'contract'. This unequivocal evidence of the context of the parties' written contract was arguably lacking in *ProForce*.

The impossibility of dispensing with context

Entire agreement clauses cannot, of course, completely dispense with context in the identification and interpretation of contractual obligations.[62] Given the limitations of language and the inabilities of contracting parties (and lawyers) always to say clearly exactly what they mean, context will always have a role. In a contract dispute, a court hardly ever confines itself to an examination of only the written documents, even if such documents appear to be comprehensive and include an EAC. However, the breadth of the context considered will vary from case to case. Judges that limit themselves to the written documents may be acting out of fidelity to what they perceive as their role and the requirements of contract law. However, a completely acontextual approach to interpretation is rare. A related reason for the inability to contract out of context is the impossibility

---

61 Cf. *Hotel Aida v Golden Tulip* [2004] EWHC 1012, at [94], where the presence of an EAC in a contract was one reason (among others) why an additional letter was not intended to have contractual effect.

62 Per Lord Wilberforce, *Reardon Smith Line* [1976] 3 All ER 570, 574. See, also, Lord Steyn, 'The Intractable Problem of the Interpretation of Legal Texts' in *Commercial Law and Commercial Practice* 123, 124–5.

of producing a complete written document that can cover all possible contingencies, that is the impossibility of producing an 'entire' contract.

These are compelling arguments and it would be absurd to claim that an EAC can render context completely irrelevant. An EAC will have little effect on interpretative disputes that hinge on the meaning of words, except in so far as it seeks to exclude certain kinds of evidence from the inquiry (for example 'necessary consent' in *Canterbury Golf International Ltd v Yoshimoto*); or that result from poor drafting (*Investors*); or evident errors on the face of the document (*Mannai v Eagle Star*); or genuine ambiguity (*The Karen Oltmann*). But these examples do not exhaust the vast array of interpretative disputes. As the above discussion illustrates, an EAC may disable the court from giving effect to implicit understandings through some of the traditional mechanisms: collateral warranties and recognition of customary understandings through implied terms, for example. Such clauses may interfere with interpretation in so far as these mechanisms are understood as means of giving effect to particular interpretations. An EAC can also restrict the contextual evidence available to the judge in interpreting the agreement. Interpretation of contractual documents is almost always about finding out what *obligations* the parties have undertaken to each other. The written document, in stating where the obligations are to be found and limiting the source of the obligations also determines in part, if not wholly, what those obligations are. The EAC is interpretative in that it is concerned with the meaning of obligations and the whole contract in a broad sense, rather than the meaning of words. It may have an important role in the identification of the obligations undertaken, which is, in the end, the *aim* of contractual interpretation.

Of course this view that an EAC posits an interpretative theory that puts the parties in control cannot answer whatever general policy arguments may be used to undermine an EAC. It will be difficult to surmount the general suspicion that surrounds the use of terms like this. Contextual interpretation and implication rules may have a role in motivating action and channelling the behaviour of contractors, as well as setting economically efficient defaults that the parties would have formulated themselves had they had the relevant resources and information.[63] The courts may refuse to allow for the general efficacy

---

63 Woodward, 'Neoformalism', 981–2.

of EACs in some circumstances. They may wish to ensure that the parties take care during the negotiating process, and do not make misleading or incorrect statements that are relied upon, but which do not take effect as collateral warranties because of the operation of other contract terms. But in commercial contracts the circumstances in which such interference are required must be rare. The justificatory hurdle the EAC must surmount cannot be as high as in a consumer contract. The line between legitimate negotiating behaviour and unfair advantage taking in a commercial contract can be very difficult to draw.[64]

Pushing the interpretative enquiry a stage back?

In the end, whether the EAC should be taken seriously is a matter that can only be determined by the context of the agreement. Therefore, one can argue that an EAC does not dispense with contextual interpretation; it simply pushes the interpretative enquiry a stage back. Katz maintains that this argument is overstated. He argues that this prior enquiry as to interpretative approach is much more limited than those contextual enquiries aimed at working out the parties' substantive obligations.[65] The kind of questions to be asked in relation to the preliminary enquiries would be similar to those used in the approach to exclusion or limitation clauses in commercial contracts – were the parties of equal bargaining power, did they receive legal advice, what were the characteristics of the contract? Who is performing or administering the contract – the original parties or others? Was it one where formality was expected (for reasons discussed in Chapter 4), and so on? If an EAC is to cut down on enforcement costs then the rules in relation to them must be clear – to save the litigation costs involved in deciding the initial validity of the clause.[66] While the linguistic and philosophical arguments in support of any particular interpretative approach are important, it must be recognised that not all parties will want a particular interpretative approach to be followed and may seek to exclude its operation. An EAC can give some indication of the approach that the parties wanted the courts to take to their

---

64 See, the Court of Appeal decision in *George Wimpey UK Ltd v VI Construction Ltd* [2005] EWCA Civ 77, [2005] Build LR 135.
65 'Form and Substance', 523.
66 Lightman J expressed such concerns in *Inntrepreneur v East Crown* at [21].

documents. But like all boilerplate terms its inclusion must be the result of reflection by the parties and conscious choice, and not just a matter of automatic inclusion by lawyers.

Conclusion

The process of contractual interpretation encompasses many techniques and methods by which the courts attempt to give effect to the agreement that the parties have made in situations where what has been agreed is a matter of dispute. The courts have eschewed literal or conventional approaches to interpretation in favour of a broader contextualism. This is in keeping with other developments in modern contract law that seek to give effect to the reasonable expectations of the parties rather than just unreflectingly enforce the written statement of terms. This revision in approach recognises the undeniable fact that every agreement exists within a particular social context, and that the legal regulation of agreements often proceeds on the basis of some artificial grounds and assumptions. Nevertheless, there are limitations on how helpful context can be in interpretation, as well as continuing debates concerning how contextual material should be identified and how effectively judges can use it. It may be that, in relation to the issue of how legal regulation of contracts is best achieved, the courts are in a period of transition. The difficulties may at root be a manifestation of the problem of trying to impose legal order on a social phenomenon (agreeing and exchanging) that does not follow any particular pattern or model. Contracts and contracting parties are endlessly variable, and in the end very few will choose the courts to settle their disputes about the contract. Those that do will have expectations of how the court will resolve their dispute. These expectations will likewise vary between contractors. To the extent that contextualism provides a methodology that can take account of these differences in reaching outcomes tailored to the contracting circumstances of the parties, then it is to be welcomed. But if contract law is to remain a facilitative and supportive institution for the parties, the courts must remain mindful of the fact that in the end, commercial parties should have as much control over interpretative method as they do over other terms of the contract.

Bibliography

Adams, J. and Brownsword, R., *Key Issues in Contract*, 1995, London: Butterworths.

—— *Understanding Contract Law*, 4th edn, 2004, London: Sweet and Maxwell.

Atiyah, P.S., 'Judicial Techniques and Contract Law', in *Essays on Contract*, 1988, Oxford: OUP.

Baker, P.V., 'Reconstructing the Rules of Construction' (1998) 114 *LQR* 54.

Barnett, R.E., 'The Sound of Silence: Default Rules and Contractual Consent' (1992) 78 *Virginia L R* 821.

Baron, J., 'Law, Literature and the Problems of Interdisciplinarity' (1999) 108 *Yale LJ* 1059.

Beale, H. and Dugdale, T., 'Contracts between Businessmen: Planning and the Use of Contractual Remedies' (1975) 2 *British Journal of Law and Society* 45.

Ben-Shahar, O., 'The Tentative Case Against Flexibility in Commercial Law' (1999) 66 *Univ Chi L R* 781.

Berg, A., 'Thrashing Through the Undergrowth' (2006) 122 *LQR* 354.

Berger, K.P., 'European Private Law, Lex Mercatoria and Globalisation', in A. Hartkamp, M. Hesselink *et al* (eds), *Towards a European Civil Code*, 3rd edn, 2004, Nijmegen: Kluwer, 43.

Bernstein, L., 'Merchant Law in a Merchant Court: Rethinking the Code's Search for Immanent Business Norms' (1996) 144 *Uni Pennsylvania L R* 1765.

—— 'The Questionable Empirical Basis of Article 2's Incorporation Strategy: A Preliminary Study' (1999) 66 *Uni Chi L R* 710.

—— 'Private Commercial Law in the Cotton Industry: Creating Co-operation Through Rules, Norms and Institutions' (2001) 99 *Michigan L R* 1724.

Binder, G. and Weisberg, R., *Literary Criticisms of Law*, 2000, New Jersey: Princeton University Press.

Bowers, J.W., 'Murphy's Law and The Elementary Theory of Contract

Interpretation: A Response to Schwartz and Scott' (2005) 57 *Rutgers L R* 587.

Brownsword, R., 'After *Investors*: Interpretation, Expectation and the Implicit Dimension of the "New Contextualism" ', in D. Campbell, H. Collins and J. Wightman (eds) *Implicit Dimensions of Contract*, 2003, Oxford: Hart, 103.

—— *Contract Law: Themes for the Twenty-First Century*, 2nd edn, 2006, Oxford: OUP.

Campbell, D., 'The Relational Constitution of Contract and the Limits of "Economics": Kenneth Arrow on the Social Background of Markets', in S. Deakin and J. Michie (eds), *Contracts, Co-operation and Competition*, 1997, Oxford: OUP, 307.

—— 'Reflexivity and Welfarism in the Modern Law of Contract' (2000) 20 *OJLS* 477.

Campbell, D. and Harris, D., 'Flexibility in Long Term Contractual Relationships: The Role of Cooperation' (1993) 20 *J. Law and Soc* 166.

Canaris, C-W. and Grigoleit, H.C., 'Interpretation of Contracts', in A. Hartkamp, M. Hesselink *et al* (eds), *Towards a European Civil Code*, 3rd edn, 2004, Nijmegen: Kluwer, 445.

Charny, D., 'Non-legal Sanctions in Commercial Relationships' (1990) 104 *Harv L R* 375.

—— 'The New Formalism in Contract' (1999) 66 *U Chi L R* 842.

Chuah, J., 'The Factual Matrix In The Construction Of Commercial Contracts – The House Of Lords Clarifies' (2001) 12 *ICCLR* 294.

Clarke, M., *The Law of Insurance Contracts*, 3rd edn, 1997, London: LLP.

Collins, H., *Regulating Contracts*, 1999, Oxford: OUP.

—— 'Objectivity and Committed Contextualism in Interpretation', in S. Worthington (ed.), *Commercial Law and Commercial Practice*, 2003, Oxford: Hart, 189.

—— *The Law of Contract*, 4th edn, 2003, London: Lexis Nexis.

—— 'The Research Agenda of Implicit Dimensions of Contracts', in D. Campbell, H. Collins and J. Wightman (eds), *Implicit Dimensions of Contract*, 2003, Oxford: Hart Publishing, 3.

Collins, H. and Campbell, D., 'Discovering the Implicit Dimensions of Contract', in D. Campbell, H. Collins and J. Wightman (eds), *Implicit Dimensions of Contract*, 2003, Oxford: Hart, 25.

Craswell, R., 'Do Trade Customs Exist?', in J. Kraus and S. Walt (eds) *The Jurisprudential Foundations of Corporate and Commercial Law*, 2000, Cambridge: CUP, 118.

Cunningham, L., 'Toward A Prudential and Credibility-Centered Parol Evidence Rule' (2000) 68 *Uni Cincinnati L R* 269.

Davenport, B.J., 'Thanks to the House of Lords' (1999) 115 *LQR* 11.

Deakin, S. and Wilkinson, F., 'Contracts, Co-operation and Trust: The

Role of the Institutional Framework', in D. Campbell and P. Vincent-Jones (eds) *Contract and Economic Organisation*, 1996, Aldershot: Dartmouth, 95.

Lord Devlin, 'The Relationship between Commercial Law and Commercial Practice' (1951) 14 *MLR* 249.

Dworkin, R., *Law's Empire*, 1986, London: Fontana.

Epstein, R., 'Confusion about Custom: Disentangling Informal Customs from Standard Contractual Provisions' (1999) 66 *U Chi L R* 821.

European Commission, *Communication from the Commission to the Council and the European Parliament on European Contract Law*, COM (2001) 398, [2001] OJ C255/01.

—— *Communication from the Commission to the European Parliament and the Council, a More Coherent European Contract Law: an Action Plan*, COM (2003) 68, [2003] OJ 63/01.

—— *European Contract Law and the Revision of the Acquis: The Way Forward* COM (2004) 651.

Lord Falconer, *Opening Speech for European Contract Law Conference*, Mansion House, Walbrook, London, 26 September 2005, available at http://www.dca.gov.uk/speeches/2005/lc150905.htm (last accessed 10 January 2006).

Farnsworth, E.A., ' "Meaning" in the Law of Contracts', (1967) 76 *Yale LJ* 939.

Fish, S., *Is There a Text in this Class?*, 1980, Cambridge, Mass: Harvard UP.

—— *There's No Such Thing as Free Speech: And it's a Good Thing Too*, 1994, New York: OUP.

—— 'There is no Textualist Position' (2005) 42 *San Diego LR* 629.

Fried, C., *Contract as Promise*, 1981, Cambridge, Mass: Harvard UP.

Fuller, L., 'Consideration and Form' (1941) *Col. LR* 799.

Galanter, M. and Edwards, M.A., 'The Path of the Law Ands' [1997] *Wis LR* 375.

Gava, J., 'The Perils of Judicial Activism: The Contracts Jurisprudence of Justice Michael Kirby' (1999) 15 *J Contract L* 156.

Gava, J. and Greene, J., 'Do We Need a Hybrid Law of Contract?: Why Hugh Collins is Wrong and Why it Matters' (2004) 63 *CLJ* 605.

Lord Goff, 'Commercial Contracts and the Commercial Court' [1984] *Lloyd's MCLQ* 382.

Greenawalt, K., 'A Pluralist Approach to Interpretation: Wills and Contracts' (2005) 42 *San Diego LR* 533.

Greenfield, M., 'Consumer Protection and the Uniform Commercial Code: The Role Of Assent in Article 2 And Article 9' (1997) 75 *Washington U L Q* 289.

Hart, H. L. A., *The Concept of Law*, 2nd edn, Oxford: OUP, 1994.

Lord Hoffmann, 'The Intolerable Wrestle with Words and Meanings' (1997) 114 *SALJ* 656.

Hunter, H., 'The Growing Uncertainty about Good Faith in American Contract Law' (2002) 20 *J of Contract Law* 31.

Lord Irvine, 'The Law: An Engine for Trade' (2001) 64 *MLR* 333.

Kaplow, L., 'Rules versus Standards: An Economic Analysis' (1992) 42 *Duke L J* 557.

Katz, A.W., 'The Economics of Form and Substance in Contract Interpretation' (2004) 104 *Col LR* 496.

—— 'The Relative Costs of Incorporating Trade Usage into Domestic versus International Sales Contracts' (2004) 5 *Chi J Int'l L* 181.

Kramer, A., 'Common Sense Principles of Contractual Interpretation (and how we've been using them all along)' (2003) 23 *OJLS* 173.

—— 'Implication in Fact as an Instance of Contractual Interpretation' (2004) 63 *CLJ* 384.

Kraus, J. and Walt, S., 'In Defense of The Incorporation Strategy', in J. Kraus and S. Walt (eds), *The Jurisprudential Foundations of Corporate and Commercial Law*, 2000, Cambridge: CUP, 193.

Law Commission, *Law of Contract: The Parol Evidence Rule*, 1986, No 154.

Law Commission, *Unfair Terms in Contracts*, 2005, No 292.

Lewison, K., *The Interpretation of Contracts*, 3rd edn, 2004, London: Sweet and Maxwell.

Linzer, P., 'The Comfort of Certainty: Plain Meaning and the Parol Evidence Rule' (2002) 71 *Fordham LR* 799.

Macaulay, S., 'Non-contractual Relations in Business: A Preliminary Study' (1963) 28 *American Sociological Review* 55.

—— 'Relational Contracts Floating On A Sea Of Custom? Thoughts About The Ideas Of Ian Macneil and Lisa Bernstein' (2000) 94 *Northwestern Univ L Rev* 775.

—— 'The Real Deal and the Paper Deal: Empirical Pictures of Relationships, Complexity and the Urge for Transparent Simple Rules', in D. Campbell, H. Collins and J. Wightman (eds), *Implicit Dimensions of Contract*, 2003, Oxford: Hart, 51.

MacCormick, N., *Legal Reasoning and Legal Theory*, revised edn, 1994, Oxford: OUP.

—— *Rhetoric and the Rule of Law*, 2005, Oxford: OUP.

Macneil, I., 'Relational Contract Theory as Sociology: A Reply to Professors Lindenberg and de Vos' (1987) 143 *J. of Institutional and Theoretical Economics* 272.

Macneil, I., *The Relational Theory of Contract: Selected Works of Ian Macneil*, D. Campbell (ed), London: Sweet and Maxwell, 2001.

Marmor, A., *Interpretation and Legal Theory*, 2nd edn, 2005, Oxford: Hart.

McGowan, M., 'Against Interpretation' (2005) 42 *San Diego LR* 711.

McKendrick, E., 'The Interpretation of Contracts: Lord Hoffmann's Restatement', in S. Worthington (ed.), *Commercial Law and Commercial Practice*, 2003, Oxford: OUP, 139.

—— *The Creation of a European Law of Contracts – The Role of Standard Form Contracts and Principles of Interpretation*, 2004, The Hague: Kluwer.

—— *Contract Law: Text, Cases and Materials*, 2nd edn, 2005, Oxford: OUP.

—— 'Review of K. Lewison, The Interpretation of Contracts' 121 (2005) *LQR* 158.

McLauchlan, D., 'Common Assumptions And Contract Interpretation', (1997) 113 *LQR* 237.

—— 'The New Law of Contract Interpretation' (2000) 19 *NZULR* 147.

McMeel, G., 'The Rise of Commercial Construction in Contract Law' [1998] *Lloyds MCLQ* 382.

—— 'Prior Negotiations And Subsequent Conduct – The Next Step Forward For Contractual Interpretation' (2003) 119 *LQR* 272.

—— 'Language and the Law Revisited: An Intellectual History of Contractual Interpretation' (2005) 34 *Common Law World Review* 256.

—— 'Interpretation and Mistake in Contract Law: "The Fox Knows Many Things . . ." ' [2006] *Lloyd's MCLQ* 49.

Mitchell, C., 'Contract: There's Still Life in the Classical Law' [2003] *CLJ* 26.

—— 'Leading a Life of its Own? The Roles of Reasonable Expectation in Contract Law' (2003) 23 *OJLS* 639.

Murray, J., 'Contract Theories and the Rise of Neoformalism' (2002) 71 *Fordham L R* 869.

Nelson, C., 'What is Textualism?' (2005) 91 *Virginia LR* 347.

Lord Nicholls, 'My Kingdom for a Horse: The Meaning of Words' (2005) 1 *LQR* 577.

Patterson, D., 'Interpretation in Law' (2005) 42 *San Diego LR* 685.

Patterson, E.W., 'The Interpretation and Construction of Contracts' (1964) 64 *Columbia LR* 833.

Peden, E., ' "Cooperation" in English Contract Law: to Construe or Imply?' (2000) 9 *JCL Lexis* 1.

Perillo, J., 'The Origins of the Objective Theory of Contract Formation and Interpretation' (2000) 68 *Fordham LR* 427.

Posner, E., 'The Parol Evidence Rule, the Plain Meaning Rule and the Principles of Contractual Interpretation' (1998) 146 *Univ Pennsylvania LR* 533.

—— 'A Theory Of Contract Law Under Conditions Of Radical Judicial Error' (2000) 94 *Nw U L R* 749.

Posner, R., *Law and Literature*, revised edn, 1998, Cambridge, Mass.: Harvard UP.

Raz, J., 'Intention in Interpretation' in R.P. George (ed.), *The Autonomy of Law*, 1996, Oxford: OUP.

Schauer, F., 'Formalism' (1988) 97 *Yale LJ* 509.

—— *Playing by the Rules*, 1991, Oxford: OUP.

Schwartz, A. and Scott, R.E., 'Contract Theory and the Limits of Contract Law' (2003) 113 *Yale L J* 541.

Scott, R.E., 'The Case for Formalism in Relational Contract' (2000) 94 *Northwestern Uni L R* 847.

—— 'The Death of Contract Law' (2004) 54 *Univ of Toronto L J* 369.

Simmonds, N.E., 'Imperial Visions and Mundane Practices' [1987] *CLJ* 465.

Simpson, A.W.B., 'The *Ratio Decidendi* of a Case and the Doctrine of Binding Precedent', in A.G. Guest (ed.), *Oxford Essays in Jurisprudence*, 1961, Oxford: OUP, 158.

Smith, S., *Contract Theory*, 2004, Oxford: OUP.

—— *Atiyah's Introduction to the Law of Contract*, 2005, Oxford: OUP.

Staughton, C., 'How do the Courts Interpret Commercial Contracts?' (1999) 58 *CLJ* 303.

Lord Steyn, 'Written Contracts: To What Extent May Evidence Control Language?' (1988) 41 *CLP* 23.

—— 'Does Legal Formalism Hold Sway in England?' (1996) 49 *CLP* 43.

—— 'Contract Law: Fulfilling the Reasonable Expectations of Honest Men' (1997) 113 *LQR* 433.

—— 'The Intractable Problem of the Interpretation of Legal Texts', in S. Worthington (ed.), *Commercial Law and Commercial Practice*, 2003, Oxford: Hart, 123.

Stoljar, N., 'Interpretation, Indeterminacy and Authority: Some Recent Controversies in the Philosophy of Law' (2003) 11 *J Pol Phil* 470.

Stone, M., 'Formalism', in J. Coleman and S. Shapiro (eds), *The Oxford Handbook of Jurisprudence and Philosophy of Law*, 2002, Oxford: OUP, 166.

Sunstein, C., *Legal Reasoning and Political Conflict*, 1996, New York: OUP.

—— 'Must Formalism be Defended Empirically?' (1999) 66 *Univ Chi L R* 636.

Sunstein, C. and Vermeule, A., 'Interpretation and Institutions' (2003) 101 *Mich L R* 885.

Treitel, G., *The Law of Contract*, 11th edn, 2003, London: Sweet and Maxwell.

Vermeule, A., 'Three Strategies of Interpretation' (2005) 42 *San Diego L R* 607.

Vogenauer, S., 'A Retreat from *Pepper v Hart*? A Reply to Lord Steyn' (2005) 25 *OJLS* 629.

Vogenauer, S. and Weatherill, S., 'The European Community's Competence to Pursue the Harmonisation of Contract Law – an Empirical Contribution to the Debate', in S. Vogenauer and S. Weatherill (eds), *The Harmonisation of European Contract*, 2006, Oxford: Hart Publishing, 105.

Weinrib, E., *The Idea of Private Law*, 1995, Cambridge, Mass: Harvard UP.

Whitford, W., 'Relational Contracts and the New Formalism' (2004) *Wis L R* 631.

Wightman, J., 'Beyond Custom: Contract, Contexts, and the Recognition of Implicit Understandings', in D. Campbell, H. Collins and J. Wightman (eds), *Implicit Dimensions of Contract*, 2003, Oxford: Hart, 143.

Woodward, W., 'Neoformalism in a Real World of Forms' (2001) *Wis L R* 971.

Index